God Loves Fun

God Loves Fun

His Holiness
Sri Sri Ravi Shankar

JAICO PUBLISHING HOUSE
Mumbai • Delhi • Bangalore • Kolkata
Hyderabad • Chennai • Ahmedabad • Bhopal

Published by Jaico Publishing House
121 Mahatma Gandhi Road
Mumbai - 400 023
jaicopub@vsnl.com
www.jaicobooks.com

Author: His Holiness Sri Sri Ravi Shankar

GOD LOVES FUN
ISBN 81-7992-369-X

First Jaico Impression: 2005
Third Jaico Impression: 2005

Printed by
Rashmi Printers
31, New Islam Mills Compound
Currey Road (E), Mumbai-400 012.
E-mail: tiwarijp@vsnl.net

Vandeham Sacchidanandam Bhedatitam Jagadgurum
Nityam Purnam Nirakaram
Nirgunam Svatmasarva Samsthitam

Asatoma Sadgamaya
Tamasoma Jyotirgamaya
Mrtyorma Amritangamaya
OM
Shanti Shanti Shantihi

I bow down to the Universal Teacher
Who is Absolute Truth, Pure Consciousness, and Bliss
Who is beyond all differences
Who is ever Full, without attributes, formless
Who is all-pervading and ever centered in the Self

Lead us from unreality to reality
Lead us from darkness to light
Lead us from death to immortality
OM
Peace, Peace, Peace

Other Works by the Author

Wisdom for the New Millennium
Celebrating Silence
Bang on the Door
An Intimate Note to the Sincere Seeker (Vol. 1 - 7)
Narad Bhakti Sutra
Quotes from Sri Sri Ravi Shankar
Timeless Wisdom

The teachings of Sri Sri Ravi Shankar are available in the form of books, video recordings and audiotapes. For a catalog of products or materials and to order, contact:

Vyakti Vikas Kendra, India – Publication Division
No. 19, 39th A Cross, 11th Main, 4th T Block, Jayanagar
Bangalore - 560 041
Phone: (91) 080 - 30622473
Fax: (91) 080 - 28432832
email: vvkpress@bgl.vsnl.net.in

May these words of the infinite illuminate your intellect, touch your heart, provide practical guidance for your life, and bring you to the playful love and laughter of the Divine. Have fun, for God loves fun!

Contents

Chaper 1

God Loves Fun

When we realize the futility of words, then we should know that our life is going deeper. We have started living.

We live in words from morning till night. Everything should make sense to us. Everything should be purposeful. In this run of searching for purpose and purposefulness, we lose all purpose. It is like the carrot and the rabbit. It is right there, still it is not there. It goes to such an extent that we don't even have a sound sleep. Even at night we are bothered by words. Many people speak while sleeping. There does not seem to be a rest from words.

Words are the root cause of worries. You can't have a worry without words, can you? Now, worry for ten minutes, but don't use a single word. You cannot! We get caught up in words. Our friendship is based on words. Someone says, "Oh, you are so wonderful, you are beautiful, you are so kind-hearted; I have never seen a person like you in my life. I have been looking for a person like you all my life." You fall in love suddenly. And when someone hurls some abuses on us, we are overshadowed. But those are just words.

Life is very shallow if we base it on words. Anything that is very profound in life, deep or meaningful, cannot be expressed in words. The experience of love, or true gratitude, cannot be expressed in words. Real beauty, true friendship has no words.

Have we ever sat, just in silence, with somebody whom we love? Do you remember? No, we open our mouths. We start chatting and we destroy all the beauty that is there. We go on a picnic and see a beautiful spot and we keep talking. You drive in a car and see how many conversations go on in the car. There are four people and two conversations are going on. Sometimes all four people are talking! Nobody understands each other. Everyone is just waiting to talk. They don't even listen. If one stops, then the other starts; they may not even wait till the other stops.

Do you remember having driven silently with somebody in the car, just looking at the beauty, the sunset, the hills, the ocean? No. We fill our minds with noise. The greater the agitation inside, the harder the music outside because then it feels a little soothing. You can forget all that inner noise, the chattering that is going on inside. Get lost in the music, that is the easiest thing. It could be a temporary relief, a soothing factor. The finer the level of consciousness, the more stress-free the consciousness, the more sensitive you are to the sound. We have become almost insensitive to noise, to sound, to words.

With the silence inside, you can hear the birds and the timing between their singing. It is so perfect, so melodious. It is such a wonderful phenomenon in creation! A bird sings in rhythm. Have you ever observed this? Without any drums, any beats, they sing in rhythm. We don't have that much patience, that much time to enjoy the song of a bird. Go a little deeper and there is a music going on very much within your own body. The divine music is happening in our own bodies. We are not aware of it.

Words are very shallow. The day we realize words are incompetent, we have gained some depth in life. We are going deeper into the existence. What do you want from your friends? Their words, their saying nice things to you or just their presence? We don't know because we have never thought what we want from our friends! "Company", we say. You know, you can be with your friends and not say a word and get into ecstasy. Both of you, or all of you, can get into ecstasy. Such a joy just being in silence! You can understand each other perfectly well, being in silence.

Your presence speaks what you are. A great philosopher may give discourses on love, but you would not feel that. It could be mind-blowing for a while, but something does not happen inside, something does not get kindled.

If you are just there, being in love, it catches on to everyone.

You may have heard many seminars on love and what happens? These people who give the seminars, look into their lives. Is there love? A lady in Los Angeles gives many programmes on love. This lady gives workshops on love and she has been divorced three times! She felt so miserable. There was so much tension in her. I said to her, Why don't you just sit within yourself, meditate, keep some silence and experience that you are love. You are made up of a substance called love. Transcend the words, then love appears." We don't allow our minds to go a little deeper, to sink into our Self. How can love flower then? It was a great day for her. Be simple, innocent, and all gets done through that power of love.

The same thing with beauty. When you look at beauty, something in you happens. "Haaa…," as though some life energy which was blocked, just opens up, like a spring opens up. A thrill, joy! Then you want to possess that! You see a nice girl, or a nice boy, somebody good-looking with beautiful hair, a beautiful nose, beautiful eyes and all nice features, and something shakes up in you. You say, "Haaa…, beautiful!" You feel so good. Then the next run is – we want to possess that beauty. The moment you possess the beauty, you make it ugly. You see men with beautiful wives who are still looking for some beautiful girls outside. Women with beautiful husbands are also still looking for some other beautiful men somewhere. May be they have broader shoulders or a long nose or good teeth, whatever they think their husband or wife does not have. Where is the end to it? The moment you possess that, you make that also ugly. There is no more charm in it. Then you go on to another, and the whole life is a run after such a mirage, a search after that. If you don't search, then you feel dead, like a log of wood. There is no joy. There is no charm. There is no beauty in life. Everything is gone. What next? There is no run. When there is no run, life seems to be very dull. There is nowhere to go.

When you see beauty, you worship, surrender to it. If we don't surrender to the beauty, we want to possess it. Whatever we surrender to, we don't want to possess it. We can't possess it. How can you possess something that is greater than you? God is conceived as beauty, the most beautiful. When you worship beauty, the sense of possession will simply vanish. Beauty is youthful. For most of us, God means an old man, somebody very ancient, with a white beard. God is ever youthful. To me, God is very naughty and God loves fun! All this is fun. That's why God created so much fun around, including all the worries and that tape that goes on with it. That is also fun. Life is fun.

When you recognize this, then life is not dull. Then spiritual practices will not be dull. Some think of spiritual practice as being very serious. You sit with a long and grim face. The grimmer the face, the more spiritually evolved the person is. The more paraphernalia they have, the more evolved they are. This is erroneous.

True experience of beauty can dawn in silence. See, we label things. Then we think we are loving. Many people think they love their lovers, but nothing is happening inside. That love, which was there initially, has disappeared somehow. To keep that fountain of life deep inside alive, one has to take some space, go deep into oneself.

There was a German boy who could not get along with any girlfriend. This was his problem He would make friends very easily and in a few days it would all break up. He didn't know what the reason was. But he talked too much, always non-stop talk. He wouldn't allow the other person even to answer. He would ask a question and he would answer it himself. He would ask the next question and again answer it himself. It was very natural that nobody could stand this. You would have to buy earplugs or simply run away. Okay, it didn't matter if other people had earplugs or not because he was not expecting answers from them. He just wanted to talk.

Well, in some programme, he met an Italian girl. The Italian girl didn't know German and he didn't know Italian. So they got married and they are still married. I told them, "It is good that you don't learn each other's language. You are fine the way you are." Whatever he needed to communicate, he had to look in the dictionary, word by word, and tell her. It took some time, and at least he could breathe and she could breathe.

We can communicate in silence very well. We can communicate through our hearts very well. There is so much in it. There is so much beauty we are missing in our lives if we have not lived in that area of silence within us. Everyday keep everything aside and stand and just look at the sky for ten minutes. Look at the stars. Look at the roses. Don't say, "This rose is beautiful; this one is big and that rose is bigger." It is there, that is it! It is beautiful. There is so much to life!

Beauty leads you to God, to gratefulness. If you see beauty and if gratefulness arises in you, then surrender has happened. Love has sprung.

Question: How can I get the courage to lose control?

You think you are in control of yourself? This is an illusion. What is in your control? Is your heart in your control? Are your thoughts in your control? Is your body in your control-let alone the environment? You can't do anything about them. Nothing is in your control. You don't need to be afraid of losing anything. It's an illusion.

There is a story about Mullah Nasruddin. Mullah Nasruddin had a dream. In the dream he was bargaining to buy a car. "I'll give you one thousand, nine hundred and ninety eight dollars," said Mullah. "No, no," said the dealer. "Then I'll give you one thousand, nine hundred and ninety nine dollars." "No, no," said the dealer. "Two thousand dollars is the final price." While this argument was still going on, Mullah woke up. He felt so bad, he said, "Such a nice deal." He suddenly closed his eyes again, "Okay, now I'll give you two thousand dollars. I don't mind paying you one dollar more. You give me the car. Let's do the deal now." A dream world. Even in a dream there is possessiveness, because that has sunk so deep in us. Just know that it is not in your control. Nothing is in your control. Then the fear of doing something about it will just disappear. So you don't need a lot of courage to lose your control. Just relax.

We think we are holding the roof. Things happen by themselves. This is a little revolutionary. May be it may raise many questions in your head, but thoroughly examine this statement in your life. All the events that have happened just fell into place for you to be where you are just now. You see the entire phenomenal world is happening on its own. You only have to watch.

Question: When you say that all one should really do is observe life, does that mean that if we don't get our own way in life, that this is how it should be?

You see, that is a thought. You want to arrange your life in a particular way. So when some thought comes spontaneously and you see that thought is right, you act on it. But you can never know that before the thought arises. You can only think what you know. When you know, what is the need of thinking about it? Thinking is the cause of worry.

You hear so much about the power of positive thinking. I tell you, this is the cause of depression. People who are into positive thinking for three, four years, they get into depression in the fourth year. Because they are thinking, "Oh no, no, think positively, think positively." The more you try to think positively, the more you are drawn towards negativity.

People are not really aware of the very mechanics of what the psyche is, what the Being is, what the mind is. You try to think positive and see if it leads to positive thoughts. It creates more negative thoughts deep within you. Somewhere in you it starts boiling up. The fear comes and your mind is divided into two. One says, "Be positive. I will be healthy." What healthy? You are unable to do something. Somewhere your consciousness is slipping down. In your mind you are trying to say, "I am healthy, I am healthy," and deep inside something else is cooking. Fear is coming up, all sorts of duality and conflicts arise.

It happened to one lady. This lady had this positive thinking, "I'm happy, I'm happy, I'm always happy and nothing can touch my happiness." And it so happened, her son died in an accident. When a son dies, a mother is not happy. Now she became very unhappy, but her old habit continued, "Oh no, I am happy. Nothing happens to me, so what. My son died, so what, I am happy, I am divine, I am bliss." She would say that for five minutes, and then for the next five minutes she would cry. It became such a big problem in her. Positive thinking had damaged her so much that she could not see the reality as reality. I said, "Don't worry about your happiness. You mourn, you cry, you weep, you be with your sadness for some days." When she whole-heartedly cried and went through the process, it was a big relief for her. Then she could really be happy. She could really feel it.

The power of so-called positive thinking might seem to be doing some good in the beginning. It touches you only on the surface level but pushes all that garbage underneath the carpet. How long can it stay there? For a day, two months, one year or two. You will find everything fine and wonderful, "Oh, it works." And then you see, underneath the carpet, it starts stinking. Lots of garbage comes up. We don't need to think positive. We don't need to think negative. We have to transcend the thinking, understand the thinking. Thinking is like a cloud in my space. They come and go. Watch and observe and you will see you will get onto another plane of existence. That is the true you. That is freedom.

Question: Punditji, in our activities we experience negative thoughts which come up. I understand what you are saying as far as the value of not pushing them down. However, don't we have a choice of whether to favour positive thoughts or negative thoughts? Shouldn't we make the choice to favour positive thoughts?

Now see, when can you choose if they have already come and gone? A positive thought has come and gone away. A negative thought has come and it has gone. When something has gone, there is no meaning in choosing them.

Question: Sometimes we hold it, though. We have a choice to hold the thought.

Now, this very choice, or our thinking we have a choice, is a bondage. Choice means a confused state of mind. You will not choose when your mind is clear. It is like saying, "I have a choice either to go through the wall or through the door." When I am clear, I would say, "No, I will go through the door." There is no choice. So when you understand that something is beneficial for life, it will automatically come. We don't say, "Okay, I will choose between unhappiness and happiness. I'll choose between being loved and being hated." Do we? Is there any choice for us? Would anybody here like to be hated? This is an illusion. It makes our bondage stronger thinking that we have a choice. Whatever is life-supporting, whatever is evolutionary, when you are clear, you will go on that path. No doubt about it. When you are confused, whatever you choose will be wrong because you are confused.

What do you call willpower and destiny? When a thought rises in your mind and that thought is according to what is happening, you say, "It is my willpower. I willed it and it happened." When you get such a distorted thought in your mind and it is against what is happening, then you say, "It is my destiny." Do you see that?

Can you will without thinking? What is a will? What is willing? It is a thought. You call it willpower or destiny. Volumes have been written on destiny and willpower and the correlation between them. But the simple truth has not been understood that they are mere thoughts. They are floating thoughts in the consciousness.

Question: Where does psychic precognition or using something like cards or the I Ching or astrology and so forth, in a predictive manner, fit if everything is kind of choiceless?

When you go a little above the time-space, beyond the thinking mind, then you can see the past, present and future, the whole time scale. It is like a big city. When we are sitting down here, we don't know the whole city. When you get on an aeroplane, you can see the whole city. You can see where the car starts and where it is going. You can see the roads, the whole highway. In a similar way, the whole vision of life can be had from a higher plane. That is where one can very definitely say that there is nothing called willpower or destiny. What is, is. And what happens, happens.

That brings great freedom.

Question: How can I trust myself more and more, regardless of what others think?

I tell you, mistrust yourself. You don't need to trust yourself and you don't need to trust anybody else. People all along have told you, "Have trust!" It has not worked. So I tell you, mistrust everything. You can't trust anything in the world. Someone who in the past told you, "Oh, you are so beautiful, you are so wonderful," today will say you are ugly. They will hurl abuses at you. People, with whom you have spent years, will suddenly one day start saying, "We have never understood each other; we never went together." What were you doing all the twenty years? Twenty years it took you to realize that you were never together at any time? It is very strange.

You can't trust anything. All the laws in the countries are changing. Russia is turning to be more democratic. Who knows? The United States of America might turn to communism. Nobody could ever imagine Russia could become more open. Last year, the year before last, and today, things are different. Countries and systems you cannot trust. People around you, your own husband or wife, you cannot trust. Your children you cannot trust. Your neighbours you cannot trust.

Your own senses you cannot trust. Your senses deceive

you every minute. You look at the sun. The sun appears to go up and down. It appears to be going around the Earth. It is not so. Your eyes give you wrong information. If you keep a pen in a beaker of water, it appears to be bent. Your eyes very clearly see it bent, and you know it is not bent. Your eyes deceive you. You eat something sweet and then drink tea with sugar in it. How your tongue deceives you! It says, there is no sugar in this tea! You can't trust your tongue!

You can't trust your ears. Your ears say it is very silent, but there is so much noise in the room. All the radio stations, all the electromagnetic waves are passing through. Only, our sense of hearing is limited. It gives you wrong information about silence and noise.

Our sense of touch deceives us. In school, did you ever try the experiment with hot and cold water? You take two bowls of water, one very hot and one very cold. Place your hands in them for one or two minutes, and then reverse your hands. The cold water will be hot and the hot water will be very cold. You cannot trust your sense of touch. You cannot trust your own mind. You cannot trust your own body. You cannot trust your own stomach. It feels good, so you eat two pizzas and two ice creams, and the next day you are in bed. You were fine the day before but now you are sick.

You can't trust your own body. This very body-which

you make such a big fuss about, cleaning it day and night, perfuming it, putting on nice clothes, is going to deceive you one day. It is going to simply drop you, isn't it? Don't feel hurt if somebody, your girlfriend or boyfriend, has let you down. Your own body is going to let you down! You want to live more, you want to do things, but your body doesn't allow you to do it. Some people, who have been very active all their lives, when they become old, become very unhappy. They have never experienced rest, never understood the value of rest and silence. They want to be active but their bodies don't agree, don't allow them to be active. They become very unhappy. This is the result of being so busy throughout life.

So you can't trust anything. Either you go to total trust, and trust everything, or trust nothing. It leads you to the same point.

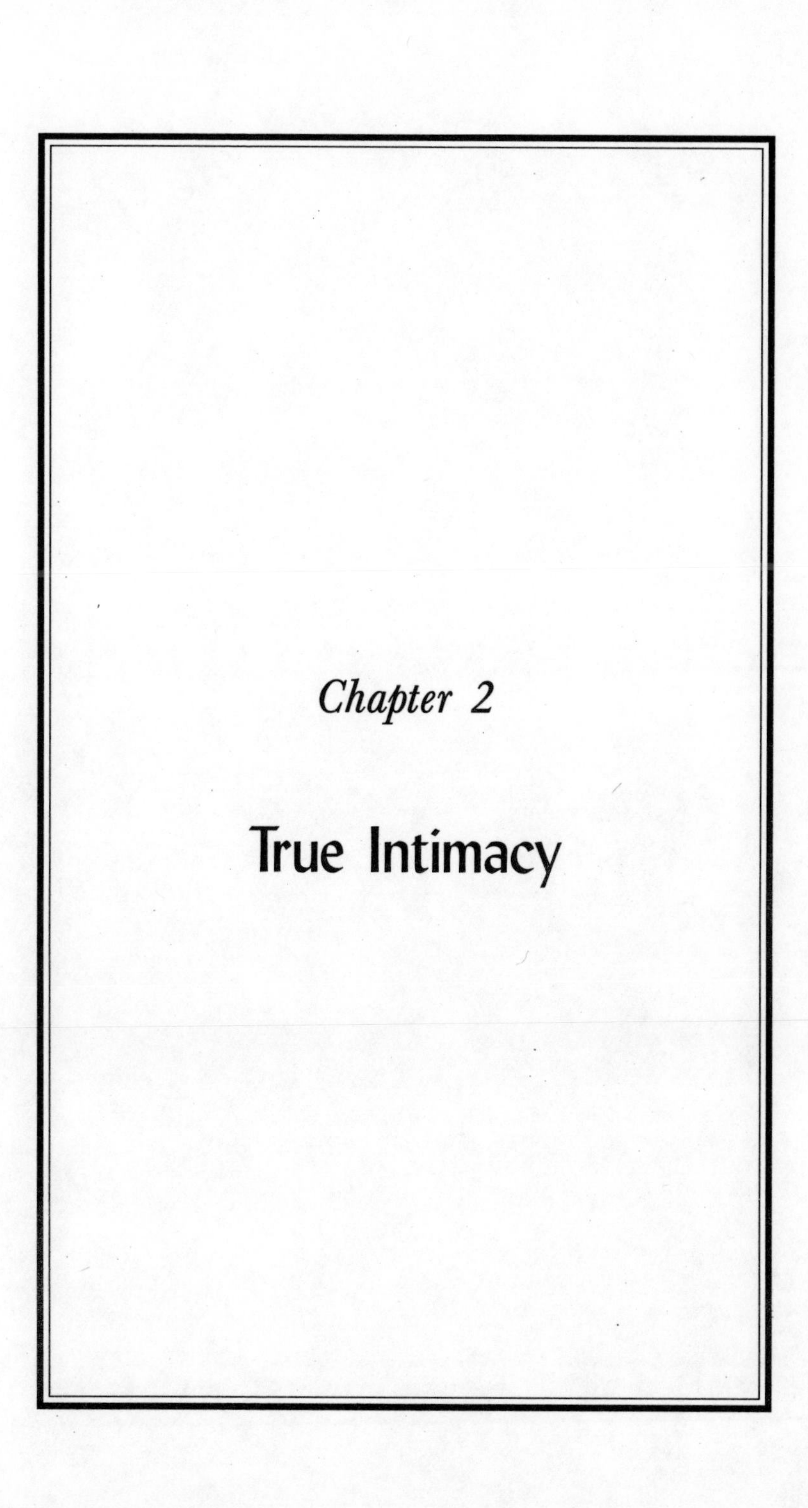

Chapter 2

True Intimacy

Question: Could you speak on true intimacy

True intimacy. When a bud breaks, it becomes a flower. When a heart breaks, it becomes divine. A flower cannot break. What breaks is the bud. And it breaks for good. What you thought was love, was not love. In true love there is no heartbreak. A broken heart means broken demands, broken expectations, broken hopes.

How can love break? Love cannot break. Can water break? Water is fluid. Love is fluid. Whatever is fluid is not brittle. Something that is stiff is brittle. It can be broken.

Life is a totality. It is like a stream. It carries the leaves, sometimes a log, sometimes a frog, sometimes swans, sometimes fish, sometimes dirt, all the industrial waste, everything. It doesn't mind. Does it say, "Oh, you are a flower, I will carry only you. You are dead logs, I won't carry you?" It doesn't make any distinction. If you pour wonderful things, such as milk, into the water, it will carry that, too. You place a flower there, it will carry that. You throw rubbish into it, that will also be carried off. Life is a stream like that.

Don't give much attention to happenings. If you give importance to happenings, if you cling to the past, then you remain there. It becomes like a stone. Then you sink.

Events are like stones. They just stay there. You be light. You let go. Don't even bother. You brush over the stones. You go away. Life is full of events, some pleasant, some unpleasant, some good, some not good. Many times you were doing something and, unintentionally, people got hurt. You want to take more care that others don't get hurt, and, in spite of that, they get hurt. Sometimes, out of your unawareness, you hurt people. The same thing is true with other people also. Sometimes, out of their own cravings, they hurt you. And so they feel heartbroken or you feel heartbroken. This is not the nature of a mature mind or of a mature love.

So, when you meet the friend again, or ex-partner, talk to them as though nothing has happened in the past, as though this is the first time you are meeting them. You don't need to give any explanation. Okay, you were partners for some time, then something happened, whether your wanted it to, or not. You moved apart. So what! Again you reach out to them, talk to them. Be friendly from your side as though nothing has happened. There is no enemy to you in the world. Live as though you have no enemies.

Our difficulty is that we express our love too much. So when we express our love too much, after a while we find there is nothing more to express. You have expressed everything. It has emptied. You may say, "Oh, you are beautiful, I love you so much." But they are just words, thoughts. Nothing is happening inside. Something is not flowing there, we are not sincere. So we try to give an idea to the other person, "Yes, I really love you." When it is not flowing, you try to show them that you still love them and that more love is happening there. But you know very well that something that had happened before, is no longer there. So we just recognize this fact.

We don't say, "They are responsible for my love." I am responsible for my love. I feel loving today. Tomorrow I don't feel loving. Yesterday there was more love. What is happening in me? This is something which is happening inside me. The other person is not responsible for it. Focusing on oneself is the path of evolution. Then one can ponder, "How can I be in love all the time, every minute of a day, all my life!" Then one clears that heavy load on the heart and the mind from inside. Then more love flows. That love becomes divine, like a blossomed flower, like this big, beautiful flower. So when you find love elsewhere, you tend to think about them all the time. You are attending to them, trying to preserve their intimacy with you, or trying to show how intimate you are with them. All these efforts of proving your intimacy with the other person is the cause of the problem.

There is no need to convince so-and-so, "I love you so much." If they understand, they understand. They may take a few more days. By trying to convince somebody, we turn the boat upside down.

True intimacy is when you feel you are already intimate. You don't try to prove it to somebody or try to become intimate. You can't become any more intimate than you are.

So when love is expressed too much, it will be short-lived. It is like a seed. You have to plant it and keep it under the ground. Never express it too much. You love somebody in such a way that they don't really know you love them. Keep it as a secret, "I won't tell so-and-so that I love him. I'll keep it as a secret." Then what will happen? Your love will flower in your actions. By saying it so much, "Oh, I love you, I love you, I love you," you destroy that.

An enlightened person may not say, "I love you so much." In the very presence, you can feel the love. In the very breath, you can experience love. In the very look, you can experience love. In any word spoken, you will hear that it is full of love. The very existence is love. That is enlightened love. That expression has not just happened in words but has manifested in matter. Now, where you sit, that place is filled with the vibrations of love. The sofa absorbs it. The chair, cloth, carpet, the entire atmosphere absorbs that love.

True intimacy is knowing that you are already intimate and relaxing about it, never trying to convince others that you are intimate, never trying to express yourself too much.

For a seed to sprout, first it has to be sealed somewhere inside. Then it sprouts. True intimacy is a combination of all emotions and feelings. Everything will be there. There can only be two things in the world-one is indifference, another is love. You can be indifferent to somebody, or you can love somebody. Love can take any flavour. You can be angry with someone and there is love there. See, you only get angry at people whom you love. You won't be angry at someone on the street with whom you have no connection. When you have something to do with somebody, when you relate yourself with someone, then you get angry at them.

So two things are there – indifference and intimacy, or love. Indifference means inertia, like a table. When indifference has died in you, you see that every one of us is connected. We are all intimate. So we don't try to connect ourselves. We are very natural.

See, you know some people for a long time, maybe several years, and then you meet them again. They don't remember you, but you remember them. How will you deal with them? You tell them, "Oh, I know you from long ago!" They say, "What do you mean? I don't know you." Do you get what I mean? The dimensions of understanding are different. I tell Michael, "Oh Michael, I know you so well, don't you remember me? Come on!" He says, "No, I really don't know you, Punditji. Only last year I just met you." He will think, "Oh, Punditji is a little crazy." So what do I do? I simply wait. I don't say, "Oh, Michael, I know you so well. You know, too. Remember, remember? I want you to remember!" I keep quiet. I am not anxious that Michael should know that I know him, that he knows me or that he should remember.

Your anxiousness to make somebody know you intimately, destroys your intimacy. This is very important. You feel intimate with somebody, don't be anxious to show them that you are really intimate with them and you really care for them.

Question: What do you do?

You simply smile. You acknowledge, you smile and allow them to become intimate by themselves. The nature of intimacy is that it wants the response from the other side. When you feel intimate, you would like the other person, also, to feel intimate with you. But they need to take some time. They need to breathe. Don't be in a hurry to express your intimacy. They may feel suffocated.

It is always so. Make them flower in intimacy from within. That will happen when you wait, when you relax. True intimacy is not in a hurry, it's not anxious. It relaxes, it knows.

Some people cannot handle the love of their partners. There is nothing wrong with their partners. But love is so much that they feel suffocated. Day and night, they won't leave them or give any space to them. That is what I call expressing your love too much. Then your actions become weaker. The charm in love is lost. So love should flower in the Divine.

A newly-wed couple was in one of the big courses. The husband would never even meditate. He was always looking at his wife to see whether she was meditating or not. He would come and ask about her experience in meditation. He was always concerned whether she was experiencing anything or not, whether she was doing the Kriya or not. She is not the wife only. She has other roles to play, too.

So, what is true intimacy? True intimacy is to take for granted that you are intimate. They belong to you and you to them. Don't make an effort to convince the other person that you love them. And do not doubt, even a little, whether they love you or not. Take it for granted. "Yes, everybody loves me." Do you know what will happen? Even if there is no love, if there is some doubt, all that disappears. This is the secret.

I know when people meet me they are friendly, but they have lots of doubts rolling in their heads. I don't take any notice. I simply know they are a part of me, that's all. I don't make any effort to know that. I know it. They are a part of me. They belong to me. It is like my own fingers. If one of your fingers is long or short or bent, you don't mind, you accept it. You don't say, "I have a thick finger, I have a thin finger, I have a long finger." You don't cut them off. You have scratched your eyes many times with your own fingers, haven't you? You have hurt yourself with your own fingers. You never chopped them off. You just take it as a part of yourself.

Question: What is self-inquiry?

Self-inquiry is seeing everybody as stuffed rag-dolls. Nobody has any fixed personality. They are all rag-dolls.

Don't see people as definite personalities. All personalities change. A good person, due to your own karma or vibration, can say something wrong to you if you have to be hurt. If you have good karma, even the wrong person will start helping you and be kind to you. This is true. I have seen people, who have committed a number of crimes, do such noble, wonderful work. They have really helped people.

Outside Delhi, thirty-five kilometres away, there is a village which was known for a very famous criminal. One day this criminal walked into the ashram with five or six others. We were about a hundred people, with pundits chanting. The criminals came there with knives and guns, but they spoke to our people so kindly. Everybody was frightened, almost fainting. Their hearts were beating and they were perspiring with worry about what was going to happen. We were thinking we were so isolated, there was no telephone, no proper communication with Delhi, thirty-five kilometers away.

Our people were so frightened when these criminals walked in, but they said, "Oh, you are doing wonderful work. We will do anything for you. We will support you. Whatever you want, we will do it in service to you." They behaved and spoke very kindly. You could see their kind hearts even in their roughness and surrounded by weapons. So others react to you in the manner that is due to you. They are all rag-dolls.

A wonderful person, or a nice person, may say something to you that would hurt, but in fact, nobody can hurt you. It is your own. So true intimacy is to see that no other person exists. It is me sitting in the form of Michael there, sometimes a little confused, sometimes worried, sometimes happy. It is me sitting there as Jeff. It is me playing all these different roles. It is all me! That is self-inquiry – not to see the difference. See, this body is a little close, that body a little farther away. That is the only difference. The Being is only one. So when the mind recognizes this oneness, the mind dissolves, disappears. This is all me, a part of me. Jeff is a part of me, Lloyd is a part of me, Shirley is a part of me.

Now look that you are there also. This body is a little nearer, that body is a little farther away. And even this body is going to drop some day. You will realize when the body drops, you will remain, "Oh, my God, what has happened? I see this body, and there is no difference between that body, this body, or this body." But if we can realize that when we are alive, that is enlightenment, that is true love. That is all there is. There is no difference, everything is me, everything is part of me.

We are in one ocean called life. All different bodies are shells containing the same water. So this name and form is an illusion. It is only relative existence. I don't mean that if I have eaten, it is enough and there is no need for Jeff to eat. No, no! In your relative work and experience, the difference is there. But in reality, for all the true values in life, there is no difference. So satsang is feeling that so-and-so is my own part. Then you have trust and confidence in yourself and in everybody. And you don't keep worrying what so-and-so is thinking about you, what George is thinking about you, what Jeff thinks about you, what Michael thinks about you, what you should do to make them feel comfortable. All this nonsense will disappear. There is so much nonsense, trying to make somebody feel better or think better. You will relax!

That is true intimacy. You take it for granted that you are intimate with everybody. You can't help but be intimate in the true Self, in reality. You may act for some time as though you are not, but it is not true. You are already connected. And don't expect a recognition of intimacy from the other person. That will destroy your own intimacy. If you think, "Does Lloyd also feel the way I am feeling, or is he feeling differently?" The very doubt in your mind will make you start observing things. You back out. So, you don't care how Lloyd thinks. Whatever he does, you feel intimate with him. It's his problem. You feel he belongs to you, so behave in that fashion. If you have to get angry, get angry. If you have to slap him, slap him. You do whatever you feel is right. That's it! That doesn't mean you don't care or consider. You do, but all this becomes very spontaneous. And your action will not, in any way, be a reaction to his response.

In true intimacy you never look for any response from the other person. It is a responseless phenomenon. That is intimacy. If intimacy needs a response, it becomes a business. Don't look for any response. You be loving, be a lump of love. You sit, talk, walk, do anything. That is freedom.

Question: What does karma have to do with the process of letting go of the ego? How do you let go? What does it have to do with karma?

That is where you need to feel the connection with the Enlightened Ones. Your connection with the Enlightened can destroy any karma. When you feel you can't let go and there is a burden, that is when you surrender. That's where you say, "Oh, my dear teacher, you help me, take this burden off me!" When you can't let go, that is exactly where your teacher comes into play. You will see the burden simply vanishes.

Question: You mean just in the presence of the teacher, or do you mean at any time?

Yes, any time. Mentally, within your mind, in your heart.

Chapter 3

The Four Approaches to Practical & Spiritual Life

A wise man is said to have four things. Both inwardly and outwardly there are four techniques. They are called Sama, Dana, Bheda and Danda.

To deal with people in the world, to be wise in the world, the first thing you use is Sama. Sama means in a peaceful and understanding way. When that doesn't work out, then you go to the second method as the rescue.

The second method is Dana. Dana means allowing it to happen, forgiving, creating a space. When people don't recognize your generosity in allowing them space, then the third principle comes, Bheda.

Bheda means to create a discrimination, make a difference, intentionally create a gap. If somebody is at loggerheads with you, first you talk to them. All problems arise because of lack of communication. If you communicate properly, talk to them with love, evenness starts. When that doesn't work out, then, with the same love, you just ignore them. If somebody makes a mistake, then ignore their mistake. Don't take notice. Allow them to realize it for themselves. Your generosity, your letting go, should make people realize their mistake. If they don't notice even then, then you start using difference, Bheda-create a difference. If two people are there, then you be partial to one person, because, by doing that, the other person will realize the mistake he has made.

In Dana, don't create any difference. It is a very big thing to note. In life you deal with Bheda many times. You create difference. But it is not with awareness or intention. It is coming out of your unconsciousness. Consciously create a difference. This, a sensitive person will understand.

Now, even then, if they don't come to the way, then take a stick, Danda, the final approach. If that person is insensitive even to the difference, what can you do with him? You have to take a stick. At last, with a stick, you make them realize.

The same four methods apply to your inner life, your Being. However, in inner life, it is not one after another. Sama, equanimity, maintain the equanimity. If pleasant sensations come, so what. Watch them. If unpleasant sensations come, so what. Watch them. Take it into equanimity. Meditation, yoga, all that is pertaining to Sama-equanimity in the mind, inside. But observing equanimity becomes difficult for many people.

Then Dana. Dana means giving up that which disturbs you, that which cannot put you in the royal seat of equanimity. What is it that disturbs you? A guilt feeling of doing something wrong or an egoistic feeling of having done something great. Both these feelings, this whole mind, with all it's merits and demerits-give it away, surrender, Dana.

You have noticed in those moments when you have surrendered, there is such a freedom. Dana is to surrender the very mind which is the cause of your sorrows, your problems, your misery. Guru Dev used to say, "The world needs your body and your possessions, I need only your mind. Give the world what it needs, give me what I need. Give me your mind." You go in the world and tell anybody, "I have a wonderful mind, will you keep it? Don't ask me anything, but I have a very beautiful mind." Nobody bothers about your mind. Guru Dev said, "I am asking you for that which nobody wants." It has the lowest value in the market. The cheapest thing you can buy today is a human mind. And even when you spend some money on it to repair it, people don't want to take it. You give your mind, you are also giving your psychiatrist fees on top of it. "Will you please take it?" People say, "No, you keep your garbage."

Your mind is your problem. It bothers you. It says, "You did good things," Which pumps you up. It says, "Oh, you did bad things," and it pushes you down. What have you done? A thought came and you were unaware and you acted. Another thought came, you were aware and you now thought, "Should I act or not act?" And that is a thought. So it is all happening by your nature. If there was tension inside, the tension brought out negative actions. If you were relaxed and free inside, it brought out positive actions. It doesn't make any difference.

Negative actions give you suffering, but that suffering never stays all the time. It gives you some suffering and it vanishes. Positive actions give you some pleasure. After some time, that vanishes. Any action, and its fruit, vanishes. It can never stay all the time. Whatever good actions you have done have their time limit, and then they vanish. It is like buying a ticket for the movie. You buy a ticket and go and sit in the movie. Whatever the movie is, a tragedy or a comedy, it is going to end. However good or bad the movie is, it is going to end. The only thing is, when the movie is not good, you have the freedom to walk out of it.

You have purchased the ticket; you have entered the theatre. Now you are yelling and crying, "This movie is bad." I say, "Walk out!" This is knowledge. Whether you want to continue staying or not, you will come out of it anyway. It has just begun. Another two, three hours you will stay, and then you will walk out. You will come out and again you will buy a ticket for the same movie the next day. This is forgetfulness. You forget from which theatre you came out, which movie you saw. You are in line again, for the same movie, hoping you will see a better movie. This is what happens.

Dana, that is surrender. Surrender is the most misunderstood word in the world today. Surrender is not slavery. Surrender is not something you can force upon someone. Surrender is a happening. Surrender happens out of love, gratitude and trust. When there is fear, drop the fear. The dropping of the fear happens with the trust, and that is surrender. If doubt still remains, do nothing, just watch. Breathe, meditate. That will clear your doubts out. There is no other way to come out of your doubt.

Four types of doubt will arise in your mind. The first doubt is about yourself, "I don't think this is for me. There is still time for me. I think I should go very slowly. Maybe it is not the right time. It doesn't suit me at all, I am not the person for it. I can never have it. I have my old patterns. I will never come out of it." These things, doubting the very self, doubting your ability – what do you know about your ability? You have no knowledge about your ability. So you doubt your own abilities.

And there is doubt about the technique. "Is this technique approved by so-and-so? Is this technique proper? Is this from some tradition? Is it a right technique? Will it do some harm to me?" You doubt the very technique.

And then there is doubting the teacher. This teacher says, "Watch the breath, be aware!" And we think, "Is he aware? Is he watching the breath? He doesn't seem to be doing that, he seems to be watching us!" You doubt the teacher.

And, finally, there is doubting your success, doubting your own experience. There was a gentleman who came to one of the courses. He was confused about everything. I asked, "What experience did you have?" "I don't know," he said. I asked, "Okay, did you have good rest?" He said, "I don't know." I said, "Are you tired?" He said, "I don't know." I said, "There could be only one thing, either you are tired or you are rested." He said, " I don't know." I asked, "Are you here?" He said, "I don't know." The real joke is that he did not even know that he was there. I said, "You are enlightened. You take it from me." Doubting whether you had that experience; "Is it true or not. Is it my imagination or what is it? Will I be able to achieve success?" This is doubting the experience.

These four doubts can hamper our progress. And when these doubts come in the mind, then surrender that mind. Drop it, "Okay, I am going to give up the very mind." It is such a weight on your head!

About judging: How can you judge? You judge from your own consciousness, from your own state of awareness. So whatever you see in the other person, you are seeing in yourself.

A person who was very egoistic, fought with everybody else. He came and told me, "Punditji, you have collected all big egos around you." I said, "How did you know that? You are seeing yourself in other people. You are egoistic and you see everybody else is egoistic. Okay, I understand if one person is egoistic, two are egoistic, or three. But if you find all the people around me egoistic, it is your own ego." And he was known for his egoistic nature.

The mind sees through its own eye. You can trust anything in the world except your doubting mind. It will doubt you. When such a thing comes, dropping that is called surrender, dropping the judgements.

Dana, the second aspect of inner growth, is very important-giving. Giving includes forgiving also. Without surrender and without love, your meditation will be dry. You can learn one hundred and one techniques. You can go on collecting technique after technique. People say, "Oh, I know this technique. I have done this before." Anything you are doing again, which you feel you have done before, you have never done. When you do something, it should appear fresh. Every day you are new.

Love makes your practice fresh and new. It is love

which nourishes, pushes forward your technique, your progress, your growth. You don't say when you love somebody, "Oh, it is an old love I am experiencing today. I have loved for so many years. It has become old and stale." There is one thing that is ever fresh and new. That is love. Any technique you do, do it with love. Even if you simply hold a stick, love the stick in front of you. It is your breath. Love is very essential. Your memory can block and arrest your love.

When your mind wanders around, allow it to go. Don't try to hold it back. Don't try to force it. Where it goes, let it go. Follow it and bring it back. This is Dana, forgiving. Not saying, "Oh, my mind is full of nonsense. I am sick and tired of my mind. My mind makes me feel jealous and I don't want it. It is very bad!" Don't start hating your mind. Forgive your mind. Say, "It is out of ignorance that my mind is going into such stupid things." Then you are not creating a fight with your mind. In most of our problems, the main problem is that we fight with our mind.

Now comes Bheda. Bheda – differentiate, separate the imperishable from the perishable. This very body is so hollow and so empty. We never realized before that inside our body there is so much emptiness! The whole body could be put into a small envelope. When you are watching the body, pleasant sensations arise, unpleasant sensations arise. As you watch, they all disappear.

Enlightenment is not just having some sensations. What has happened? Many people go and do different types of kundalini. They try here, there, raising this chakra, raising that chakra. What are they doing? They are just playing with some sensations. You can do it with acupuncture. Acupuncturists will put needles in different places. You can yell and shout and have the energy move up and down. It has some utility in the sense that it energises you. It puts your mind a little bit in the present moment. But that's all. Nothing beyond that. It doesn't give you the knowledge of your Self, your Being, which is space, emptiness and the fullness.

People are having different sensations as a game. It is already happening! If you can watch, energy is oozing out of every pore of your body. If you watch, it flows in an even manner. It creates balance. And you realize you are not this body or these sensations. You have been always reacting to the sensations. You are like that, year after year, life after life. Now, when you watch, that is liberation. Watch all the feelings and sensations in your body. You go beyond. "Now, Eureka! I have found it!" What was happening? An emotion used to give rise to some sensation; the sensation, in turn, used to create an impression, another emotion. So these circles of craving and aversion with sensation and emotion, made your life, both subtle body and gross body, and that took you from life to life.

Every sensation has its own quality and nature. When

you feel pleasant, what is happening? Those sensations are moving upward. Whenever you feel unpleasant, the same sensations are moving downward. A pleasant sensation is pushing you up, an unpleasant sensation is pushing you down, Just watch it. When all the energy goes down, an unpleasant sensation occurs and your head feels fuzzy and empty.

Your body has certain centers with emotions associated with them. When you feel jealousy, joy, arrogance or attachment, you feel the sensation in the stomach. It churns your stomach. When you experience love, fear or hatred, you feel the sensation in the heart region. Grief is in the throat. There is a choking sensation in the throat. Gratitude is also in the throat. Being full of gratitude chokes the throat. You can't speak. Anger is in the forehead and so is awareness. People who are alert, get angry. Each emotion has a particular pattern of sensation in the body. Your body is enough of a thing to watch. There is no time to think about others if you could just watch your body. There is no time to think about anything else or to form any opinion about anybody.

Somebody came and asked a saint, "What do you think about this particular situation?" The saint said, "Where is the time to think about anything? I have no time to think." This statement is difficult to understand: "I have no time to think." But how can you think when you are in the present, when you are aware, when you are in the now totally? Thinking is like chewing gum. It doesn't produce anything. You can think about only those things which you know. And once you know, what is the need to think about it? And you can't think something which you don't know. How can you? It is not possible. Ultimately, thinking is useless!!!

Knowing this difference is Bheda. The third thing that you can do is differentiate between the permanence and the impermanent. Buddha said, "Look into every sensation, this is impermanent. You disassociate yourself from the sensation. What is happening in the body, let it happen." A grief is coming. He says, "This is impermanent. This is something that is changing. I shall not associate with it. I'll watch the sensation instead." It becomes very intense and disappears.

It is the same with a pleasant sensation. Hang on to it, grab it and you will see that all pleasant sensations vanish and become painful a little later on.

Bheda means seeing the permanence and the impermanence. This very body is impermanent and, with the very attention into it, you become a glow of consciousness. It is not the body-it is the glow, it's the consciousness. It is Chetana, Chitta, that is coming out of every pore of the body. There is a wick coming out of the candle. The wick is not the glow, is not the light. See, the wick is dark and ugly, but the glow is so beautiful. So are you. The wick is the body and you are the glow. Any moment you are walking, eating or sitting, just become aware that your body is hollow and empty. The body is nothing but a handful of ashes, would-be ashes. You will see, when you shift from the wick to the glow, your mind becomes stable-Bheda.

You say your mind is wandering very much. I don't think so. Mind is not wandering. It is your lack of understanding. Bheda Buddhi, this bheda is not there. You don't know what is impermanent and what is permanent. You have never put attention on it. If somebody's life is in danger and you ask them, "What do think about politics? Who do you want to vote for?" They would say, "I don't care! Rescue me!" Your mind will go according to Bheda, according to your discrimination.

Then comes Danda – Danda means support. Determination and commitment are the Danda. Your spiritual discipline is Danda. Mind is like a vine (creeper), it needs a support. Listening to spiritual discourses, satsangs, practice, Guru's presence are all the support, the Danda.

Chapter 4

Real Laughter

If you ever happened to meet God, do you know what you would tell him? "Oh, I have met you inside." God will dance in our life when the day dawns in laughter and love. The true prayer is laughing in the morning. Don't just be laughing outside but from deep inside. The laughter comes from the center of our Being, from the core of our heart. Our belly is so full of laughter that the laughter permeates and comes out of every cell of our body. True laughter is true prayer.

In nature everything is just waiting for you to laugh. When you laugh, the whole of nature laughs with you. It echoes and resounds and that is really the worth of life. When things go all right, everybody can laugh, but when everything falls apart, and then if you can laugh, that is evolution and growth.

So there is nothing in life that is more worthy than your laughter. Never lose it for anything, whatsoever. Events come and go. Some are a little pleasant, some are unpleasant, but whatever happens, they all leave you untouched. There is some area deep in you that is left untouched. Hold on to that something that is untouched. Then you will be able to keep laughing.

There are differences even in laughter. Sometimes you laugh just to avoid thinking or to avoid looking at yourself. But when you see and feel within yourself that life is so present every moment, so intense every moment and it is invincible every moment, then nothing can bother you. Nothing can touch you. Then laughter is very authentic. It is real laughter. You might have observed babies, six months old or one year old. When they laugh, their whole body is jumping and bouncing. The laughter is not just coming out of their mouths. Every cell in the body is laughing. That is enlightenment. That laughter is innocent, pure, without inhibitions, without any strain.

Someone asked me the other day, "What is your opinion about North America?" I said I had none. They said, "No, you are supposed to have an opinion about everything." I said I had no opinion. Opinion means you have an experience, you catch hold of that experience and, in the future, you see everything through that one experience. So you don't allow room for a new experience to come and reflect in its purity. My mind is like a mirror. I see whatever is, and that is what I reflect, and that reflects again and again. The moment the scene goes away from that mirror, the mirror is as it was before. It remains without any impression.

Opinions are the impressions that we make on our minds. If we have one experience repeated four or five times, fortunate or unfortunate, then for the rest of our lives we tend to see the whole life through those same glasses. What we have not been taught is how to keep our innocence, so that our minds are not imprinted with definite opinions. We need to be able to see things as they are, objectively or totally subjectively.

That essence in life, when it blooms from within, allows true laughter in life. We have all been in that state of godliness. Godliness is a feeling of belongingness. We all belong to one another.

See, now what is happening in our minds? "What next? What next?" Back-talk is happening in our mind. The mind says, "Yes, yes, no, no." Opinions come and go. Are we aware of them? Now observe what is happening in your own mind, this very moment. It doesn't matter whatever I say. You can agree, disagree, it may appeal, it may not, so what! But are you aware of this process, the phenomenon that is happening within you? Yes? That is very good. That is godliness. Godliness is within each one of us.

Laughter opens us up, opens the heart. And anytime we don't feel up to that innocence, what do we do? That is a question that comes, right? "I feel tense, I don't feel that innocent or free. What do I do?" You can attend to several layers of your own existence. First, the body – see if you have had good rest, proper food and some exercise. Then attend to the breath. Breath has its own rhythm. Every mood of the mind has a definite rhythm in the breath. By attending to the rhythm in the breath, the mind and body can be elevated.

Then look at the concepts and opinions that hover in the mind. Good, bad, right, wrong, should do, shouldn't do, all these could bind you. Observe the thoughts. And then observe the feelings. Every thought is associated with some sensation, some feeling. Observe the sensation and feeling in the body.

Observe the rhythm in the emotions – if you observe, we never make new mistakes. We commit the same old mistakes. It is simply a repetition. I never say, "Don't do any mistake." I usually say, "Do at least some new mistakes." Have a variety of mistakes. The pattern, the rhythm in the emotion is the same; situations are different. This is like the same coat, but you hang it on different hooks. You have the same pattern of emotions but you hang it on different causes, different things, people, circumstances, situations. Attend to this rhythm of the emotions. The peak of any emotion will lead you to yourself.

You get to the peak of any emotion, the height of any emotion, then it leads you to space, and you are space. It is like when you take off from the ground in any direction, you will go into space, go up above the clouds. Any emotion, height of anger, height of fear or joy, whatever, leads you to a place where you are in your centre.

There is a lot of talk about positive thinking. Positive thinking means – you get a negative thought and you try to think positive. A thought has already come in us, whether positive or negative. You just observe it. It is already gone. But positive thinking means bringing back that which has gone. We catch hold of a thought and go on like that. To erase the negative thought, we try to force a positive thought on it. But negative thoughts simply don't go away. They go somewhere deep inside. They remain there. The more you try to force the positive thought, the more, somewhere deep inside, the negative thought is growing. A slight fear is happening; you are hitting a duality, a conflict. Observing thoughts as thoughts, emotions as emotions, opens us to our true Self, the godliness within us.

Question: Do you mean just the observing from some centre is enough, rather than trying to change it?

Yes. The very observation changes it. When you observe, all that is negative falls away. And the nature of positive emotions is – they grow. If you observe when you are angry, the anger will fall away. And if you observe if there is love, love grows.

Question: And the attempt to erase simply strengthens the negative? Is that what you are saying? Just observing and letting go is the simplest?

That is the best and only way. Observe. Observe that thoughts come and they pass. A negative thought comes because of stress. If you are put under great stress, on that day, or the next day, you will get negative thoughts and become frustrated. All negative thoughts come out of your frustration. Instead of trying to do something with those thoughts that have already arisen, which are of no use, attend to the source from which they bubble up. If the source is clean, only positive thoughts come. And if negative thoughts come, you observe, so what! They come and they vanish in no time.

Question: Is it true that in India many decisions are based upon astrology? And if so, how can we learn to incorporate more of that in our lives?

I think astrology is everywhere. People everywhere look into the date of birth and month of the sun sign. All the planets affect the intellect and emotions. Beyond that is the Being and they cannot affect the Being. Being is so powerful. It's as powerful as the sun, as powerful as atomic energy. An intention from the level of Being can change the effects of all the stars and planets on our system.

Question: Punditji, talk to us about the significance of celibacy in our life.

Celibacy is a happening. When your awareness is so deeply rooted in the Being and Being is permeating everywhere, and when the thrilling joy and love is coming from every pore and cell of your body, a natural phenomenon that you call "celibacy" happens. The bliss in you is like the peak of the sex experience. When that stays with you as an electric current all the time in your body, you don't feel the body as a physical heavy body. It is light like a flower. It is like space, like air. When you get very spacey, you don't do anything. You don't feel the body because you are so immersed in joy. Then celibacy happens. It is not a practice that one does. It is a spontaneous happening, when love has flowered so much in our life.

It is one energy which, in the lowest centre of our body, manifests as sex energy as well as creative energy. See, when you are very creative, if you are going for an examination or are involved in a large business, those days thoughts of sex don't cross your mind. You work, you go to sleep and you work, because that particular activity occupies your mind so much. When you are very creative, the sex energy is transformed. People who are obsessed with sex are less creative. The one energy comes as either procreative or creative energy.

When the energy moves further up, to the second

centre of your body, beauty and the arts are enlivened. The same energy turns into arrogance and jealousy. One energy has these two aspects, either as beauty, arts and appreciation, or as jealousy and arrogance. They are not two different energies.

Have you observed our tendency with beauty? We see beauty and we want to possess it. You may see a nice crystal chandelier and say, "Oh, I want it." You bring it home. Do you enjoy looking at it every day? No. Again when you go out, you see other types of chandeliers which attract your attention. Most of you have beautiful paintings at home. Do you look at them every day or enjoy them? You seldom do that. You may say you enjoy them, showing them to guests. Do you really enjoy them? No.

Your tendency is – when you see beauty, you want to possess it. In the process of possessing it, you make it ugly. When you see a beautiful boy or a beautiful girl, you want to possess, you want to love them so much that you make it hard for them to breathe. This is happening! People are suffocated by love! And people are hurt by love! You can't get hurt if there is no love. If you love somebody and they don't smile at you or are busy, you get deeply hurt. You don't get hurt by somebody who you don't love. Hurt is a part of love. And you don't want to accept that. You just want people to love and say goody-goody things and smile. All these modulations of the mind open up and change with observation. To me, celibacy is a gift that comes to you. It is a happening.

The word celibate means 'married to God'. That means God has possessed you so much, has so fully entered into each cell, that there is no space left for anything else. Celibate means to be married to the spirit. Having seen over and over again, for life-times, what sex is, you move a step further and become immersed into That, Divinity, that love which is.

Question: You mentioned that celibacy is a happening. If celibacy isn't happening, how can sexuality or sexual union be a part of bringing about the state of Being that you're describing? How can that practice enhance that movement?

No practice can bring love in you or beauty. What is the root of sex? What do you get in sex? Joy, a thrill, some love, comfort. You know what happens in sex? An energy, which is dormant in you, gets opened up. A sensation rises all along your body for a few moments. Every cell of your body is in the present moment so totally. That is joyful. If the joy was just in the body, in the organs, it should remain all the time. It doesn't remain all the time. Your attraction dies out the moment your energy escapes or releases from your body. Now, attending to this energy, this is what real joy is. Focus on that rather than on an object on the outside.

When you see beauty, you want to possess it. Instead, you surrender to it, you love the beauty and you see that the beauty never dies. That becomes gratefulness. You look at a flower and you feel it with you heart and you surrender to the flower, instead of wanting to possess it. That is the institution of marriage.

What is marriage? It is when the husband sees the beauty in the wife and he surrenders to the wife. He says, "I trust you so fully and I give myself to you." He is not wanting to possess the wife but he says, "Now I am helpless in front of you, I am nothing. Whatever you want to do with my life, you do. I am at your disposal." And the wife does the same thing to the husband. She says, "I see you as an embodiment of beauty. Now I offer myself to you. I surrender myself to you." Mutual surrender blends into one glow of love, into total understanding.

In day to day affairs, some misunderstandings may come, anger may come, tension comes. All this is a part of life. One may get a little bit hurt, or one may get a little bit angry. Do not make each other feel guilty. If you make anyone feel guilty about any small thing, then you have created an enemy already. Never make people guilty and, yet, make them understand where the flaw has happened. This is again another art.

Sex gives you a glimpse of what the highest possibility

of your life energy could be; how you could live in vibrant love every minute.

Question: Can you tell us how we can become more and more aware of that Being that you speak of in our daily life?

I have already mentioned this – through breathing techniques and meditation, and through releasing the stresses from the system, observing nature, observing your life, observing the patterns of your body, mind, emotions and breath. One of the techniques which I usually recommend and teach in the Basic introductory course is 'Sudarshan Kriya', where you go into your breath and all these patterns and discover that you are pure joy. You say, "Oh, this is what I am!" Once you have a glimpse, you see everything is changing, changing, changing, and then you will be able to be in that state.

Question: Describe your concept of God for us.

God is beyond all concepts. It is an experience. Whatever cannot come within your concept, know that as God. The moment you make a concept, your intellect says, "Yes, I know". God is the eternal "I don't know". But you can be God. You can live in God. You cannot know God. You can experience God. Whether you know it or not, experience it or not, you are That. Every religion has said what God is, has given a general concept of God as omnipresent. If He is present everywhere, He is present in you. He is present at all times. If He is present at all times, is He present here, now, this minute? Yes? That is it. Being here now, this minute, being in touch with your innermost Self, you are in God.

Your mind is never in the present moment. It is vacillating between the past and the future. You are anxious about the future or you are angry about the past. All your anger is about the past which is gone, finished. And all your anxiety is about the future which is not yet here. The present moment is so deep, it is not shallow. Bringing the mind to the present is called meditation, samadhi. Here you are in God.

Question: At times when I've been in India, I've been struck by what you're talking about and it seems that somehow the Hindus and the vast number of deities are like this bridge to God. You have a way of having God in your life all the time. You walk down the street and you make contact. I've been overcome with that same deep feeling while I've been sitting listening to you. Somehow the concept Hindus have of God far surpasses what much of our Christian processes have led us to, because we have been left with rigidity. We've been left with an angry God who punishes. And we haven't seen that there is much more that can't be named, but can only be experienced, that is beyond that. I don't know how we make the transition in our culture today. Having been in India, walking the streets and contacting somebody with just "Namaste", suddenly I notice that there is that eye contact that's from a deep, deep pool of knowing. It makes me yearn to go back to that place. It makes me want to live in that space more, so that I can create more of it here, so that somehow that energy keeps moving around.

According to the need of the time and day, different aspects of one divinity have manifested in the world. When India was at it's peak of glory, God was conceived as Satyam Shivam Sundaram: truth, beauty and being auspicious – all that is life-supporting. People are beautiful everywhere, I see that. People are the same. Because of different stresses, tension and circumstances, a covering comes up, but that is not their nature. Beneath those coverings people are the same. People are deep and loving here, too, not only in India.

Question: Yesterday, one of the members asked you about what was happening in his life and there seemed to be lot of confusion within that person and you addressed the subject of confusion. Would you do that again?.

Confusion is thinking that joy would come better from the other way, when you have already chosen one way. Whichever you choose, you think the other will give you more joy. So in that state, you take a pillow and go to bed. Joy is not going to be better from anything. You are the source of joy.

Chapter 5

Dealing with Feelings

When we feel high, we have no problems. The problem comes when we feel low. No one wants to feel low. When one feels low, then the more one tries to feel high, the more the low feelings persist. This seems to be the biggest problem. What is important about the feelings? They never stay the same. Feelings are fluid. See, you feel good now, later you don't feel good. Then again you feel good. This continues in life. If we base our life on our feelings, we will be ruined. You feel good about something now and a little later you feel bad about the same thing. Then those feelings change yet again. Have you noticed feelings changing?

Many people are unaware of the nature of feelings. Everywhere you will hear people say, "Follow your feelings, go by your feelings, do what you feel like," etc. What will you do? Be independent? People misinterpret what independence means. They think it means following your feelings. They think, "I do as I feel now, I do as I feel tomorrow, I do as I feel the next day." Then there can be no stability in life.

We are unhappy if we follow our feelings. When you feel low, jump into the lowest. Be like water. That is your real nature; inside you, it is like water. The coconut is the symbol of the whole human life. The coconut has a husk. That is the environment. And then the shell is the body. The mind and the inner intellect is the white membrane inside. The water is the innermost part. Your true nature is like water, fluid and not hard inside. What is the nature of water? Humility, it always goes down.

Stiffness is the problem. Stiffness is ego. Water can take any shape. Whatever glass you put it in, it will take that shape. Water means acceptance of the present moment. You put the water in a bottle and it will take that shape. Our innermost Being agrees with nature. In water, the slightest movement makes ripples. It is dynamic also. It is not simply acceptance with fatalism; it is acceptance with motion, with dynamism, with readiness to jump up. A little shake, and the water is ready to jump up.

The ocean is the lowest. How has the ocean become an ocean? It has accepted the lowest. Can there be anything lower than an ocean? All rivers from the mountain tops flow down to the ocean. The ocean is full. The humblest is the greatest. If you agree to go low when you don't feel good, you will become the richest person on earth. Have you ever loved your low feelings? You have always fought with them. When you don't feel high, just close your eyes and go into that low. "Okay, today I shall agree with my low feelings and I shall go as low as I can, without acting." Do not do any action but just agree, "Okay, I am going down, down, down…." How far will you go down? You will find the ocean there. You will start rising up in no time.

Depression and low feelings cannot touch you. They can do nothing to you. However big the clouds are, they cannot overshadow the sun. It could be the darkest day, but still it will remain day, and those clouds can never make it night. So, when clouds are there, you don't have to shiver. Just go deep, observe and you will see a lot of sensations rising up. Some fears come up. What is fear? Just a sensation in the body. Agree to it, "All right, let it be. I will dive into it today." An amazing thing happens within you, a phenomenon. Psychiatrists will be out of jobs. Everybody can look into this aspect. This is very, very beautiful.

What is the nature of water? Water, when it reaches the ocean, does not always remain there. It rises high as the clouds and then comes down again as water. Feelings and water are synonymous.

There is an aphorism on love by Rishi Narada. He says, "The nature of love is extreme anguish." If you have not had extreme anguish, then you have not had supreme love, either. Then your love is also shallow. So, the higher the capacity to love, the greater the anguish of separation. That is synonymous. That is the other side of the same coin and it is fine. It is a painful pleasure. This is a stage, and only when this stage is transcended, then bliss stays. Then such a peace dawns that can never be shaken.

If you try to fight with your feelings, they take a longer time to clear. There is only one way, "Let go" or "Surrender". Why is surrender stressed so much? Always, in all religions, in all enlightened spheres, they say, "Surrender." Surrender means that which you cannot handle, keep it on a plate and offer it. What is it that you cannot handle? You cannot handle your own feelings, you cannot handle your own thoughts, your own confusion.

If you are confused yourself, how can you clear your own confusion? Is it possible? Your trying to clear your own confusion causes much more confusion. What can happen is that you can find yourself in confusion! Many people do not know that they are in confusion. The lucky ones find themselves in confusion. When we are aware of our confusion, we offer it. That is what is called surrender. Surrender means having trust in love, saying, "Oh, this is too much for me, I feel so bad, please take care of this. Relieve me of my…." You leave it to God. Then you relax.

In a subtle way, surrender is happening to you every day. Otherwise you cannot sleep. Before going to bed, all that you did, your thoughts, your desires, your hang-ups and all that — what did you do? You just dropped them and dropped yourself on the bed and your head on the pillow. Someone said, "Every night I surrender, in the morning I take it back." So, every night everybody surrenders to some degree. It is in everybody's nature. You leave everything for a few hours. Then you are happy and peaceful. You sleep well. In the morning, when you wake up, you feel light and again you carry the basket on your head.

Feelings are the same as the nature of water. Observe the creation. You can observe the phenomenon inside you. Awareness is like fire. Awareness burns. If you have no awareness, you have no burning. There is no light. Observe the intellect, mind, memory, all the inner faculties. Observation of these laws that govern our inner faculties is very essential.

There is a story about Mullah Nasrudin. His son came home from school and said, "Daddy, I got a prize in school." Mullah asked, "For what?" He said, "They asked me a question and I answered, so they gave me a prize." Mullah asked, "What is the question that they asked you?" His son replied, "How many legs does a cow have?" "And what was the answer you gave?" "I said three." "What, you said three and you got the prize?" He said, "Yes, everybody else said two, I said three and so I got the prize".

That is what psychiatrists are! They know nothing about the psyche, the mind, the consciousness. They simply drug people, make it complicated and then make you believe that your madness is a very natural thing, that there is nothing wrong.

When depression comes, surrender, bow down several times, think you are dissolving and disappearing like a candle, like camphor. Have you seen camphor glowing, how it glows, how it burns? It does not leave any trace behind. If it is pure camphor, it burns totally and disappears. Like that your whole life will burn like camphor on this earth and will disappear without leaving a trace. So many millions of years have passed and there are millions of years to go in the future.

What is a life? How many years? See with your own eyes. Open your eyes and see how time has passed like that, twenty, thirty, forty, fifty years. And in those fifty years, see how you have been tossed by your feelings. When you follow your feelings, have you ever felt peace at any time? You will see the answer is "No". So, don't base your life on feelings. Base it on commitment, conviction, truth, wisdom. And love. Base life on love and giving.

Question: You said something about not trusting your feelings as to what to do. How do you tune into your dharma? How do you know what you want to do in your life if you do not trust your feelings? How do you know the difference between the Big Mind speaking to you, as opposed to it just being feelings?

I did not say, "Don't trust your feelings." I said, "Don't simply follow your feelings". What is the nature of your feelings? When you feel clear in the mind, then naturally you have good feelings. When you are unclear in the mind, then you don't feel so good, right? Vice versa, when you don't feel good, your mind is also not clear. Any decision that you take when your mind is unclear is not going to be good for you. Instead of that, base it on just the clarity of your mind.

There could be a positive imbalance and also a negative imbalance. You went somewhere and you felt very high and you then made a decision there. Later on, you didn't stick to it or you did the opposite. When you are in your true Self, in your Big Mind, that is unexcited, calm, collected and serene, then the true commitment, direction or vision for your life arises. See that your life is always in alliance with that vision.

Vision means what? It means giving direction for life energy to flow!

Question: If you are in a state of confusion, as I am, you forget all about what vision you had. You remember there was a vision, but you forget everything like that, everything is black.

When you know that you have forgotten, that moment you have remembered, haven't you?

Question: But I do not remember what to do.

Suppose, I say, "Oh, I forgot my pen. Oh, I forgot my key." That means I have remembered it. There is no way to know that you have forgotten, when you have not remembered.

Question: What if what you forgot was a state of consciousness?

Silence will bring the memory back.

Question: Remembering it, and re-experiencing it, can be two different things. Remembering that you once had it is different from being with it again. I remember I lost my keys but I have no idea where.

Good, that is the very first step. Then you start looking for them. That is what I am saying. You are going in the right direction when you are beginning to remember. The very beginning of remembering is the beginning of reliving.

Question: Punditji, is it natural when you know you are just Being, you are just living and then all of a sudden something happens? It is as though all of a sudden you find yourself kind of lost, and you are groping to get that state back again. Is it a natural part of evolution? You have it, and you are Being, then all of a sudden you lose it and then you make your way back to it again.

Yes, very natural. That makes it more dramatic, more charming, more enjoyable.

Question: But is it not like the anguish part of love, where you remember that you had it but you don't have it now?

It is an inevitable stage.

Question: You talked about laws that govern the internal processes. Can you talk more about that?

The process has begun already. Has it not begun? Let it be, it will continue.

Question: Punditji, when you have fallen out of that state of just Being and you are trying to get back to it, is one of the secrets of life learning to love that getting to it as much as loving Being, loving the trip back to Being as much as Being itself? It would be like loving the depression as much as the joy.

Yes, Yes. When love dawns in you, all these questions do not arise at all, because then this forgetfulness will not come. When we are in joy, we forget. You forgot yourself, you become unaware when you are very happy. When you are unhappy, you are less forgetful. It keeps you in touch with the mundane but in joy you tend to lose yourself. If you don't lose yourself in joy, you will never be unhappy either. That means when you are happy, remain in gratitude. That is the only way – when you are happy, feel grateful and serve.

How can you then be unhappy? Impossible. If you are unhappy, go out and serve. You will become happy. Do some service. Unhappiness comes when you sit and think about yourself and worry about yourself. The candle is burning for you, you don't have to do anything. The sun is shining for you, there is nothing to do. You have to be grateful, sit below it and enjoy and serve and be in love. It's as simple as that.

If you want to make it without surrender, that is a very hard way. You can get it also, but it is very hard. You feel all alone. Loneliness will come, fear will come, and a lot of strain and struggle. You can do that, go through all the processes. It is very difficult. But with devotion, with love, with surrender, it very easy.

Question: Punditji, are you saying that in service we cut the negative patterns that repeat in our lives?

Yes.

Question: I find that when I am stuck and not feeling in love, when I tell myself to surrender, I really do not know what the word 'surrender' means. I don't know how to surrender. I think I'm surrendering, but then I still don't feel any different. And every time I hear you, or anybody, speak about surrender, I say, "What does that really mean?" How do you surrender?

Don't try to surrender. Your trying to surrender is an obstruction. You are already a part of the whole, just remember that. Know that there is somebody who cares for you and who is taking care of you, and you will be all right.

Your life is not your life, you see? Your life is an event in time, which is infinite. Surrender has happened when you know your that life is insignificant in the span of time and space. When you know there are millions and millions of stars – just look at astronomy books and see how big the solar system is and where the Earth is – then what is one's life? When you see this, surrender has happened! And when you know somebody is really behind you, who loves you so dearly you can't even imagine, then your surrender has happened. Feel the connection, then surrender has happened. Don't think, "I am somebody separate". When a cup of water feels, "I am in the ocean," and the water in the cup knows that "I am connected with the ocean," it gains strength. Belongingness happens. When there is belongingness, there is no fear. It cuts the root of fear.

How has fear arisen in your life, do you know? Up to

eight months children are not afraid of anything. They fall down. Even then there is no fear. At six to eight months, the child does not know any fear. Sometimes even up to three years, children don't experience fear. If they experience fear, it is due to some little traces from the mother. But when the separateness starts, when the child has to be independent for longer periods and does not get as much attention or love from the mother, then fear develops little by little. Or, parents induce fear in children.

Question: Is there an alternative way to teach a child not to touch the stove? How should one approach that without giving unnecessary fear?

Now, I didn't say that it should not have been there. It is impossible for somebody to grow in life and not know fear. At some point or the other they will know it. It will come to them. I am just making you aware of how it starts, how it was not there in the original child when it was born. I don't mean that you eliminate it or it should not be there. If you are aware, then you know it is not your nature. It can go away in life.

In India there is Kali worship. Do you know Kali? There is a great significance behind that. If you look at a Kali picture, it is dreadful. Anybody would be frightened looking at all the skulls and huge staring eyes. She holds a head in one hand and she has hands hanging all around the waist. If someone could love that fearful picture, then fear disappears from the mind. The fear gets transformed into love. Because it is only one energy which manifests as fear or love. It happens in the heart region. When you are in love, there is no fear. When there is fear, there can't be love.

So, when the fear comes, surrender. This is the best thing one can do. When you surrender to Kali and love Kali, you become very brave. There is no fear in your life. That is the concept of it. Kali means darkness. Darkness is the mother of light. There is darkness in the eye. Through that darkness, only, can we see the light. The pupil is dark in your eyes. If it is not dark, then you cannot see light. Kali is the mother, the giver of knowledge. Through Kali, knowledge awakens, light awakens. Wonderful minds brought the symbol of Kali. It is very, very beautiful. God is conceived as beauty.

Chapter 6

The Nature of God

God is the junction of presence and present. Whenever every cell, every atom of the mind and body get totally immersed in the presence and present, you experience something ecstatic, something beyond this world. An experience of eternity comes. This "Me!, Me!" dissolves. You say, "I am." This "I, I, I." You find there is nothing like "I". "Is-ness" dawns. Is. There is something. And what is that something? You don't know. That is presence. A presence where only knower remains is God.

Many people talk in terms of "God is speaking to me, I have a message from God." It is your own consciousness split into two. One part of your own consciousness becomes God, another part becomes your mind. That is not God. God is the totality. Everything is in God. There is nothing that can be outside God. Whether good or evil, both exist in God.

Which thought is there which has not come from God? Every thought is in God. The thinker is God. You are not separate from God. You cannot be separate from God, this is for sure. You can never be away from space, whatever you do. Even the worst sinner can never escape from God. God is omnipresent, and if He is omnipresent, He is present in the rich or in the wicked, as much as He is present in the wonderful. The only difference is that one knows it, another one does not. Wherever you see the difference, there is duality, the two.

In silence there is no duality. This is just a taste of being all by oneself. But you have to go deeper into the silence. Just not talking is not enough. Your mind should also be in that same space. For example, when you fly in an aeroplane, you are flying thirty thousand feet in the sky above the ground. You have left this earth. You are in space. Your little body is thirty thousand feet in the air. Just imagine! From there you see this house as though it is like an ant, almost invisible. Your body is that high, but still your mind is stuck down here. You are not totally flying with your mind. You are not keeping your mind at thirty thousand feet. Your mind is deep down, stuck in the mud. Then silence simply cannot happen.

Silence is expansion. Expansion of awareness is presence. Whenever you have felt presence, you have felt it as somebody, some things, some objects. Then the consciousness is not expanded. In deep silence, the presence is enormous, limitless.

As, during this afternoon, in one of the exercises, you started observing. What was happening? You felt you were not there!! Just the observation remained. Even only a glimpse of this is an experience of the very presence. That is God. That is the pure source of your Being from which everything has come; from which you have come and in which you will dissolve after the body drops. You dissolve into the "isness." That which "is"

Be aware of your mind. Is your mind confused, pleasant or unpleasant, loaded with anger or love? Observe this moment. What is there? Expansion is already happening. This very moment, recognition of oneness comes up. Whatever the mind is chattering, let it chatter. So what! It is a part of you, it is not the whole of you. Accept even this chattering mind, don't fight with it. Don't say, "Don't chatter, don't do this, don't do that." Then you start to struggle. This very observation, the presence is always there.

You can never meet God. When you meet God, you disappear, only God remains. Either there can be God or there can be you. In Hindi there is a couplet which says, "Prem ki gali ati sankri ja mein do na samaye." "This path of love is so narrow that two cannot be there." You and God cannot be there. Either you are there or God is there. You can never love God!!!

Can you measure water with a stick made of salt? The

moment it touches the water, it dissolves. You can never measure with it. So also you and God. In your true nature, you are God. Free of guilt, full of surrender, you are God. This is the ultimate goal of all life.

As every river goes into a big lake or into the ocean, so also, all life merges into the infinite life, the Big Life, the Big Mind. That is the goal, full flowering. Each one of you has a Big Mind, and this Big Mind contains all your future and all your past, infinite future and infinite past. The Big Mind contains all your hopes, your desires, all your possibilities, all that you can achieve in life, all that you can have. The Big Mind contains everything of you. It has all the answers for all your questions. There is nothing that is outside your Big Mind. And your Big Mind contains every other mind. It is your own Big Mind.

Every thought that comes to you comes in the mind. And the thought is spontaneous, it happens. You have no control over it. All discoveries have come out of the Big Mind, your own Big Mind. See, in your body there are so many cells, right? Each cell has got its own life. Today your body does not have the same cells which it had ten years ago. Cells have died, new cells have come up. So, a constant birth and death of cells is happening in your body. From the time you were born till today, new cells have come up, and old cells have gone. So these little cells, which have their own lives, don't know you as a whole. So also with all the different bodies. There are so many bodies here, each having its own little life. We do not know a Big Life which contains all these lives together. All our minds put together is a Big Mind, a Big Life. That life you may call God. And you are the centre of God. You are so dear to God. So there is a Big Mind and a small mind. The small mind chatters, saying something at one time, some other thing at another time, liking something now and disliking the same thing a little while later.

Somebody came to me the other day and said, "I am going to separate from my wife." I asked, "What is the problem? How long have you been married?" He answered, "Twelve years, but you see, Punditji, we never went well together a single day." But how could they live for twelve years? I said, "If you lived together for twelve years, why don't you live together for another twelve years? You suddenly discovered today that you never went well with each other for so long?"

The small mind changes. But when the small mind is unaware of the Big Mind, then it becomes unstable. The Big Mind is an expansion. When the small mind becomes silent, it becomes the Big Mind. Your experience is that whenever the small mind becomes quiet, you go to sleep. You are never aware of your Big Mind, the Infinite Mind, Cosmic Mind. Jesus said, "My Father and I are one. God and I are really one." There is this Sanskrit verse, it says, "Between God, Guru and your Self, there is no difference." It is just the name that is different, that's all.

A Master, an enlightened Guru, is one who is reflecting the Big Mind. The Guru also has small things, a small mind. Because of that He can eat, sleep, walk, talk, express-but it is transparent. He is reflecting the Big Mind all the time, twenty-four hours. As the disciple or student grows into the Big Mind, he still gets a little doubt whether something is from the Big Mind or the small mind. So, go and ask the Master. The Master will simply confirm whatever the Big Mind, your own inner pure Self says. There is no doubt about it. There is no difference. The Master is simply mirroring. You get into your Big Self, the quiet Self, the Big Mind, and whatever comes, invariably the Master will say that same thing to you. The Master is an outer reflection of your own inner Self. So when you can trust your Self, only then can you trust your Master. Or if you trust the Master, then the trust in your Self also grows.

If you cannot love somebody else, it is because you cannot love yourself deeply. If you find that is hard, start loving the Master so deeply and you will see it doesn't take you long to become the Big Mind and live in the Big Mind.

The Big Mind has all your future possibilities. Everything is in it, all that you need is in it. All that you want is there. It fulfils, it complements your little mind. The Big mind will be there, like a mother taking a baby to a big shopping centre. As she goes around, the baby wants this and that. It wants almost everything and it changes its mind. It picks up a little toy and says, "No, no, I don't want a teddy bear. I want an elephant. It picks up an elephant and says, "No, I want a duck." It goes back and forth. It gives the mother a big headache. Sometimes the mother says, "All right, you can have it." Sometimes she says, "No, come with me." She pulls the baby away by the hand. Otherwise it will bring the whole shop into the house!

In the same way, your little mind says something. Sometimes you grant it. It doesn't matter. And sometimes you don't grant it. With this very awareness, you can handle every situation. In all circumstances, you start reflecting the Big Mind. Things which you don't know will come to you. The knowledge comes spontaneously.

Sometimes philosophy students come and sit in my talks and ask me, "Where did you study? Where did you learn? Did you study books?" No! For me not more than two, three pages move. I take a book, one, two, three pages, by that time I am off. At the rate I read, it would take several thousand years to read all those books. Once in a while I pick up a book. The page doesn't seem to turn, it seems to get sticky! So I close the book. By reading, things do not work. By getting into your Big Mind, all knowledge becomes available. It is quite spontaneous.

Wherever we are, we can become aware of the Big Mind. Your small mind expands into the Big Mind. With the Big Mind your communication is so total. We can communicate with each other in silence. Be aware of the

Big Mind and see how wonderfully you can communicate. The waves are already there, only you have to tune in. The radio is also there, you only have to switch on the radio. Electromagnetic waves are already there. The receiving set is ready and you are here to switch it on. Just switch it on and you will see how you will catch it. It is so simple.

Ego is harshness, hardness. It is the "I". But that dissolves by just watching, not trying to dissolve it. If you try to dissolve it, it still remains. Many people teach that you should erase the ego or let go of the ego. This doesn't work. By just being aware, relaxing and becoming aware of the Big Mind, the ego automatically vanishes. With this, the values which we cherish in life are all there. Turn back and you will see that the whole life is like a dream. Isn't it? See the past. Is it not like a dream? Till today, till this moment? You came here, you settled; the day before you had started from somewhere. Before that you did something, something else on New Year.......you enjoyed your Christmas presents. The year before, and the year before, you cried and yelled and much before you shuttled back and forth from school for years-bored, waiting for the weekend. Isn't it? That is all gone. Is it not like a dream? Look back and see it is like a dream.

And what is going to happen? A few more days, what can happen? At the most, you will laugh and jump, or you will cry and sit. So what! Anyway, it is all going to pass, however you spend your time. Why bother so much? In order to smile and laugh, you are bothering so much.

Your effort to smile and laugh is making you cry and weep. You are doing the opposite. There is nothing you need to do. Just smile and laugh. Life has no purpose, no mission. It is a game. It's a play. Life has no message. Life, itself, is an expression of joy. There is nothing you have to do. Everything is being done by the Big Mind.

There is a story of two lizards. One lizard was up on the ceiling and another came up from the wall and told the first lizard, "Why don't you come for a walk? It is a nice sunny day outside. All winter we have been inside. Why don't we go out in the sun?" The first lizard said, "Oh, no, no! What are you saying? If I move, the ceiling will fall down. How can I move out of here? Don't you have any sense?"

This is what we also think. You make no difference in the world whether you live or you don't live. Whatever is happening, happens. Even that is not under your control. Whatever has to happen for you is going to happen.

You have this big question, what is free will, what is destiny? When things happen according to the thought that came to you, you claim it to be your free will. When your thought was contrary to what happened, you call it destiny. Very simple. People write big volumes on free will and destiny. You can open two pages and you fall asleep. For insomniacs it is a good thing. When a perfect thought comes to the small mind, you call it "free will". The small mind thinks, "Oh, how nice, it is my free will." Free will, what free will? If the small mind fights against the thought that is coming through it, it calls it destiny. What is, is!

I know I am the Big Mind. I know you are also the Big Mind. And there is no difference between you and I. I am in you. I am everywhere as Big Mind. It is all just different bodies, but one big Mind, one ocean. And all this variety in creation is your own making, your own joy.

In your life, you have chosen all events, pleasant and unpleasant. Sometimes you have been happy, sometimes unhappy. So what! Why take life so seriously? There is nothing worth taking so seriously. It is all fun, it is all a game. There is a beautiful term in India. It is called "lila". Lila means game. Life is a game. It is a play. The way it is, it is beautiful. All teachers come to tell you, "Don't take life seriously. It is a play." Awakening means, "Oh, come on, what is there, why are you bothered about that dream? You had an unpleasant dream yesterday, so what! It is finished. Now wake up this moment!" Don't go on analysing the dreams.

God is wakefulness.

Dreams are just dreams. They have no meaning. What happens? Certain past impressions in the mind are all getting released. In those moments, there may be some intuitions and thoughts from the future too. That gets mixed in. The dream is a mixture of so many things. If you start analyzing, it is a waste of time. When you awaken, your dream shatters. A dream is either in the past or taking you to the future. Either you are daydreaming or you are dreaming about the past. Past is past. Throw it out! This moment you feel the presence. Don't miss this moment. It is valuable. That is what grounds you in this moment. Now!

The concept of the Old Testament God is that God is waiting there for you to make a mistake and then hit you with a stick. The moment you do a mistake, He is on you. He takes revenge on you. He is angry at you. He is going to punish you. It is a very primitive thinking. What sort of God is He? Couldn't He correct the person before he did the mistake? Why wait for somebody to do a mistake and then correct him? What was He doing before? Sleeping? You are denying the omnipresence and the omnipotence of God by saying that.

No, God is not waiting to punish you. He is so loving. He is taking care of you every moment. God is compared to a mother, "Meenakshi". Meenakshi means that God has the eye of a fish. A fish never closes its eyes. And if it has young ones, it is always following and keeping watch on its young ones. God is called "Meenakshi", a mother. A mother never loses track of her young ones wherever they are going. And she moves with them.

See life as a game, as a play. You are God, you know it. I am God, I know it. So let us play. And when you come from that level of consciousness, there is nothing to teach. Only being. Come and sit, be with me for a while. That is enough, for you and I are one. This is love, isn't it? That is what God is telling you every day, "I am doing everything. You come and sit with me. Whatever needs to be done, I will get it done through you. You simply stop existing."

The very science of astrology is also that. See, it is all designed this way. What do you do? Relax. That is the only thing that you can do. Relax in surrender. You are in the Big Mind.

Chapter 7

Being a Fool

What is the topic? Learn to be a fool or just being a fool?

Somebody who is not doing what the crowd does, what society does, somebody who goes his special way, you call him a crazy fool. No one wants to be a fool. We resist being a fool. Who would like to be a fool? All effort in life, in society, in education, is put into trying to be wise, trying not to be a fool. Isn't it? That means just being one among the crowd, just flowing with the crowd. If somebody raises his hand, you also raise your hand, not knowing for wh:

You have something which you call social laughter. People laugh whether they understand the joke or not. They simply laugh. If you don't laugh, people will think you are a fool or you are dull. So you laugh. It is said the Englishman laughs twice. Once he laughs for the social custom. When a joke is told, he simply laughs. And the second time he laughs at night when he understands the joke. But a German laughs only once because he will never understand the joke. Somebody from Israel never laughs because he does not know what a joke is.

The day fools disappear from this world, all your entertainment will be gone. Your TV stations will have to be closed down. Fools are the greatest source of entertainment in the world. They do something special, and you laugh. The "I Love Lucy" show, does it come here also? You turn the television on and something crazy happens. They do something very funny, so you laugh. But if you saw someone really acting like that around you, somewhere in the house or in the town or in the neighbourhood, you would get mad at them.

Fools make you laugh. Fools keep you happy. Fools are very essential. God is bored with wise people. He likes fools. He loves fools. Even the job of God is very foolish. Why does He make leaves fall every autumn? He does it over and over again. The tree is tired shedding all the leaves, becoming dry, and again growing new leaves, season after season, again and again. The Creator is a bad economist. He doesn't know any economics. He wastes things. So many people are being born and they all die. And they spend thirty, forty years studying.

Einstein studied all his life. He became so wise. If God would have granted him another hundred years, he could have accomplished even more. God doesn't seem to understand it. He brings even more children into the world. It is bad economics, isn't it?

Creation is continuing. There is no aim. There is no purpose. When somebody does something aimlessly, without any meaning, without any purpose, you call them a fool.

We want to find a reason for everything, a purpose for everything. We want to analyse and understand everything. People even try to understand their dreams. What is the use? Whatever dream you have had, so what? Whether you are sitting on horseback or on top of a train in your dream; whether you see a crow or a duck or a pigeon or swan or a mouse or a cat in your dream, what does it matter? Why do you waste so much time interpreting dreams, understanding dreams, trying to know something about dreams? We call ourselves wise because we want to understand. We want to do something only if we get something out of it.

A fool is somebody who does something and doesn't get anything out of it. Their foolish acts, even those you can interpret into meaning and purpose, you see they do them without any purpose, without any meaning. Since childhood we have been told, "Don't be a fool." What is wrong with being a fool? What is wrong with standing alone, apart from the crowd? "Let the crowd act however it wants. I stand apart from that. I act my way."

God is not a communist. If God wanted to be communist, He would make every place on earth the same. There wouldn't be any mountains. It would all be even, like a desert. Everything would be the same. Yet the world is not so. The world is full of variety. There are so many different kinds of people living on this planet. Different types of noses-no two people have the same nose. So many varieties are there and such uniqueness. Not even two fingerprints match.

A fool is somebody who does something very unique, which is not accepted by others. All entertainment, including games, are foolish acts. Just think if a person from another planet, maybe Mars, comes here and sees a huge crowd watching a team of boys on this side and another team on that side, trying to fight for a ball and put it into a basket. It would appear absolutely funny! One ball in the middle, a team of boys here, trying to push it there, trying to push it that way. Why all this trouble? Why don't they just take the ball and put it in the basket? What difference does it make whether they put it in this basket or that basket? It is so foolish, playing soccer, playing basketball. For hours together other people sit there, howling and yelling and clapping. You should see the whole drama. There is really nothing in it. In cricket-somebody throws a ball, another person hits it and what do you get for hitting a ball? George Bernard Shaw said somewhere, "Cricket is a game where eleven fools play and eleven thousand watch." It is true. All games are foolish acts. A game is a game because it is foolish. If you find meaning, purpose, aim and competition, you destroy the whole game.

If you are not foolish in your life for some time if possible all the time, if not possible, at least some time-you miss your life. You miss the joy in life. If somebody calls you a fool, how do you act? Your eyes become red. You start grinding your teeth! However, it is a great compliment. You should wait for such a compliment because this is very difficult to get. People may feel that you are a fool and they often don't say it to you. If some people, with great courage, come and tell you that you are a fool, you should feel happy.

The greatest problem for us is being a fool. We try not to be fool. All our life we resist and fear arises in us. A fool is one who acts with freedom, who has all freedom, isn't it? That is how he could be a fool. If somebody has not experienced freedom, he cannot be a fool. Freedom is behind every fool. God loves you being a fool. He doesn't love wise men so much. He is bored of their theses and philosophies. He is terribly bored by all the books written about Him.

Make the whole life a game. A game means there is no purpose, there is nothing. Just take it lightly, easily. Play the game. That is worship, that is celebration. There is nothing that you do that will please God. There is nothing that you will do that will displease God. He is not waiting there with a staff, just waiting for you to do a mistake so He can punish you. Don't have such a cruel picture of God as someone who is judging, who is going to punish you if you do this or that. If He doesn't want you to do something, you can never do it. It is impossible. The very fact that He has allowed you so much freedom to do anything you like, means He says, "Don't take anything seriously, it is all a game. It's all like a dream."

Whatever has happened till today, till this moment in your life, is like a dream. You cried, laughed, shouted and got angry at somebody, threw the dishes all over your floor, made all sorts of drama, haven't you? You banged your heads against walls or banged somebody else's head. You yelled or made somebody yell at you. To God it is all fun. He is watching, it is all just a game.

See the impermanence in this life. That is the truth. Turn back and see that all that you did is like a dream. Whatever you do in the future, you may become the mayor of the town, or you may rise to the highest position, or you may have a lot of wealth, so what? You have cried and wept, got angry and agitated, so what? All has passed, the whole thing has finished. This very moment, like this, tomorrow will pass. Whether pleasant or unpleasant, it will pass.

Now and then, a pinch of unpleasantness comes. Do

you know why? It makes you aware of your pleasantness. Suppose you never had unpleasant moments in life, you would never have pleasant ones either. You wouldn't know what pleasantness is. Your life would stagnate of utter boredom. You would become like a stone. So, in order to keep you alive, now and then, here and there, nature gives you a little pinch. It makes life more lively. Accept it.

God does the same thing to you. Now and then He gives you a pinch. Then you start weeping. But just turn back and see-tell me very honestly, every time you had difficulty, were you taken out of the difficulty or not? Any time you had some problem, you got a helping hand. You were picked up. There are stories of people who were drowning in the river where there was nobody else. They don't know how they were saved.

I don't mean that you should jump into the ocean and see whether somebody takes you out. I tell you, you don't have to be afraid in life. There is always support. So, every pinch that you are having in life, is for the best, to make you life more lively and enjoyable. You see, there is no purpose in life. Otherwise why are people born and why go through all that when they are going to die one day? Is this life? Are you born just to pay your bills? If you are born just to pay your electricity and phone bills, taxes, life is not worth living.

Day and night you work so hard. You are waiting for

Friday to come. The whole week is spent madly working, coming home tired, eating, going to bed, sleeping, and the next day the same thing. And weekends also-the same routine. Weekends have become another routine, a change in routine, that is all-the same gossip, the same sitting around, drinking, the same movies and the same type of conversation.

If you're awake, then you see there is so much foolishness! Just watch when four or five people get together and talk, have a gossip session. In a gossip session, you can immediately change the topic of conversation. This is the thing with a crowd. If ten people are talking about the weather and you change the topic to stock markets, everybody will immediately talk stock markets, whether they know about them or not. And then from stock markets you change to health food. They will not have completed the previous topic but they will jump on to this topic! It is great fun.

Being aware of this impermanent nature of our life, the changing nature of happenings-you find that there is something in you that has not changed. There is a reference point by which you can say things are changing. Getting onto that reference point, that is the Being. That is the source of life. That is wisdom. A wise man is a fool. All wise men were called fools. Galileo was called a fool when he said the earth was moving around the sun.

A fool is one who is relaxed, who is free, who is happy. He is not bothered about what he gains, whether material or spiritual or whatever. What have you done with all that you have gained? Where has it led you? Nothing to gain, nothing to lose. By your doing, you are not pleasing or displeasing God. There is a saying in Sanskrit: "My original home is in heaven. I come here to rest." I have come to the world to rest and play, to watch and to see what is happening here. In this world, you just be aware and alert and watch everything that is happening around you. It is great fun.

This is a place of entertainment.

You have experienced the same patterns in your life in the past and you see the same thing repeating over and over again and again with x or y or z. Coming out of this pattern in our life, that is awareness. Be aware of the pattern first of all, and then just take a jump. Be foolish. Agree to be a fool. "Okay, I shall be a fool. Okay, I'll jump." Then there is infinite freedom in life.

Even your spiritual practices should not be a big, heavy load on your head. Your spiritual practices should be something which is done with a sense of freedom. Spiritual practices begin with love. When there is so much love, it is not an obligation. It is not something you must do, like every Sunday you must go to the church and pray. It is not a must. It is the juice in your life. The way of your life is prayer. Your very being becomes prayer. Your walking becomes prayer. Your work becomes prayer. Anything you look, at with that gratitude in your heart, becomes prayer. Stand near the ocean and look at the vastness, the depth, and all the huge waves rising in it! Something deep in your heart happens. That is prayer.

If autumn is approaching, just walk around and see all the colourful trees, all the colours in the world. Feel these blessing and be grateful in your heart. That very moment prayer has arisen in you.

The Art Of Living – We Care We Share

The Founder – His Holiness Sri Sri Ravi Shankar

His Holiness Sri Sri Ravi Shankar has been feted the world over by governments and the common man for being instrumental in helping people leading happier, healthier and stress-free lives, for being a reviver of human values and for the immense social work that has been undertaken by the Art of Living Foundation that he has created. He is also a key founder of the International Association for Human Values. Yet, beyond all these large, visible, tangible achievements he is a *guru* whose touch is personal. He has always maintained that we are here to develop the individual, not a movement. He lights the flame of love in one heart and this one heart in turn transforms another ten and these in turn transform another hundred. That is how he works, giving an opportunity for leadership and service to every single person connected to him. His compassion, joy, love, wisdom and playfulness have given a whole new dimension to spirituality.

Born on May 13 1956, in Papanasam, Tamil Nadu, India, it was apparent from an early age that His Holiness Sri Sri Ravi Shankar was destined to lead a spiritual life. As a little child, he was often found rapt in meditation and at the age of four could recite the *Bhagavad Gita*. As a young boy he would often tell his friends, "People all over the world are waiting for me." By the age of 17, he had completed his education in both Vedic literature and modern science.

In 1982, he began to teach the *SUDARSHAN KRIYA*, a powerful yet simple breathing technique that eliminates stress and brings one completely to the present moment. This is taught around the world as a part of the Art of Living course. Many people have experienced physical and emotional healing from the various programmes offered by the Art of Living Foundation.

The Art of Living Foundation – In Service Around The World

The Art of Living Foundation is a non-profit, educational and humanitarian organisation committed to creating peace from the level of the individual and fostering human values within the global community. The Art of Living service projects and educational programmes are carried out by the foundation in over 140 countries. As a Non Governmental Organisation (NGO), we work in special consultative status with the Economic and Social Council (ECOSOC) of the United Nations participating in a variety of committees and activities relating to health and conflict resolution. (www.artofliving.org)

The Art of Living Workshops – Holistic Development of Personality, Body, Mind and Spirit

The Art of Living Course Part 1

It is a simple, yet profound workshop that offers the *Sudarshan Kriya*, practical spiritual knowledge and interactive sessions. The *Sudarshan Kriya*, the very heart of the workshop is a unique breathing practice. A powerful energiser that cleanses deep-rooted emotional stresses and toxins, it brings the mind and body in synchronicity with natural rhythms. Serenity, centredness, better health, greater joy and enthusiasm for life and more harmonious relationships are just some of the results. The 15-20 hour course is spread over 5-6 days.

The Art of Living Course Part 2

The Art of Living Course Part 2 is a programme that takes you deeper into yourself... You can experience the vastness of consciousness that you really are. The Part 2 course is a vacation in the true sense of the word leaving you rejuvenated and relaxed both physically and mentally. The Part 2 course includes *Sadhana* (Spiritual Practices), *Satsang* (Spiritual communion through singing), *Seva* (Service) and Silence.

Sahaj Samadhi

This is a simple and profound manner to bring the mind to deep inner peace. Daily practice helps integrate the depth of inner silence with the dynamic pace of life. It leaves one feeling rested, relaxed and energised.

Divya Samaj Nirman (DSN)

Divya Samaj ka Nirman (DSN) means 'creating a Divine society'. If, you've asked yourself this one question: What can I do to make this world a better place, then the DSN has the answers for you. Society is a reflection of the individual and the DSN empowers an individual to contribute to making this world a better place.

ART Excel Programme (For 8-15 year olds)

ART Excel stands for All-Round Training in Excellence. A highly effective programme for children, it includes the *Kriya* to help release stresses and negative emotions such as fear, anger, aggression etc. through the breath, interactive games and various processes that develop concentration, build confidence and inculcate human values such as sharing, caring, acceptance, trust and respect.

Youth Empowerment Seminar (YES) (For 16-20 year olds)

In an age where young adults grapple with peer pressure and stiff academic competition, the Young Adults Course helps youth to inculcate a sense of belongingness, leadership and competition. It includes the *Sudarshan Kriya*, interactive processes, discussions and lively games. Among the benefits that students find are improved memory, concentration and clarity; enhanced creativity, increase in positivity and confidence and that it's a fun way to deal with stress and pressure.

Prison SMART

This is a unique stress management programme which assists prisoners in personal rehabilitation, reducing violent tendencies, while teaching inmates to accept responsibility for past actions and future conduct. The aim is to enable them to go back into society and make a fresh and happy beginning once more.

The Art of Living Corporate Workshop

This highly specialised workshop has been designed to equip a person to open up a new dimension to management skills and achieve excellence at the workplace. It offers a paradigm shift from working hard to working smart and to achieve the balance between meeting the demands of personal and professional lives. A practical and effective training programme it empowers managers and employees to experience calmness and inner clarity in the midst of challenges. It is engineered to build teamwork and leadership, through processes of self acceptance and awareness. It is based on the *Sudarshana Kriya* and other innovative breathing techniques and universally applicable values that contribute to self development, harmonious interactions and contribution to society.

Service Projects

The International Association for Human Values

While celebrating our distinct differences, the International Association for Human Values (IAHV) was founded in Geneva in 1997 aims to create a deeper understanding of the values that unite us as a human community. IAHV develops and promotes programs of personal development to encourage the practice of human values in everyday life.

In fostering Human Values, the Association works in collaboration with partners dedicated to similar goals, including governments, educational institutions, other NGOs, corporations and individuals.
(www.iahv.org)

The 5H Programme

The 5H programme was conceived by His Holiness Sri Sri Ravi Shankar in 1997 under the aegis of the International Association for Human Values (IAHV) with a special thrust on Health, Hygiene, Homes, Harmony in Diversity and Human Values. This programme is the vehicle through which a wide array of humanitarian, service projects are delivered in countries around the world. Universal in its scope, yet deep-rooted in its effects, it is a flexible programme that suits the diverse needs of different cultures. Thus, one can see the success of the 5H in diverse projects in countries like India, South Africa, Poland, Kosovo, USA, Latin America and Indonesia. And, we can see the transformation in the smiling faces of people, whether it is a farmer in Karnataka, a slum-dweller in Mumbai or a villager in war-torn Kosovo! An integral part of the 5H programme is the *Nav Chetna Shibir*. It is known internationally as the Breath-Water-Sound Workshop. It includes breathing techniques, guided meditations. The 5H areas of

focus are all highlighted in this workshop.
(www.5h.org)

Youth Leadership Training Programme

The Youth Leadership Training Programme (YLTP) forms the backbone of the 5H programme. The YLTP focuses on developing confident and dynamic youth leaders (*yuvacharyas*) who can become engines of transformation. This holistic training imparts skills for them to become socially and economically independent, while moulding them into empowered rural entrepreneurs. With their cooperation and commitment, communities worldwide are learning to strengthen at the grassroots level. These youth are instrumental in implementing the 5H programme in villages, thereby bringing about social reform along with economic independence.

Rural Development Programme

The Rural Development Programme (RDP) gives groups of young men and women the opportunity to come from their villages and spend four months in the Bangalore *ashram*. Here, they receive training in agriculture, sales and marketing, computers, dairy farming, electronics, welding, woodworking and carpentry. The programme is balanced with yoga and meditation practices as well as physical fitness training. All these disciplines help them return to take leadership roles in their own villages.

VISTA-India

VISTA-India was started by Acharya Ratnananda, father of His Holiness Sri Sri Ravi Shankar in Uragalli, Karnataka to uplift the lives of rural women. It recognises that self-supporting, happy, healthy women are the foundation for strong village communities. This programme goes into the poorest areas of rural India and provides vocational training for women in basic skills such as tailoring, type-writing, basket-weaving, incense-manufacturing which enables them to be self-sufficient. In addition they are taught reading and writing, personal hygiene, yoga and meditation. By the end of the programme the increase in their own self-respect, in their awareness, in their dignity is immeasurable.

Sri Sri Mobile Agriculture Institute

With the objective of taking agricultural knowledge to the door-step of farmers, the mobile agricultural institute was launched recently. The institute will provide guidance to farmers to become self-reliant, educate them in adopting healthy and natural agricultural practices and instil in them a sense of confidence.

Sri Sri Ravishankar Vidya Mandir

This project aims to take value-based education through schools to the tribal and rural areas of India. Since 1999, we have opened over 56 schools where uniforms, shoes, books, writing materials and mid-day meals are provided free-of-cost. The first initiative was starting a school near the Art of Living International Centre, Bangalore in 1986 for the children of neighbouring villages. This school today caters to over 800 children,
(www.srisrischools.net)

International Centers

21st km, Kanakapura Road
Udayapura,
Bangalore,
Karnataka 560 062.
Telephone: 91-80-8432274
Fax: 91-80-8432832
artofliving.org

13 Infinity Road,
St. Mathieu du Parc, Quebec
G0X 1N0.
Telephone: 819- 532-3328
Fax: 819-532-2033
artdevivre@artofliving.org

European Center Bad Antogast

Bad Antogast 1,
D - 77728 Oppenau, Germany.
Phone: 0049 7804-910 923
Fax: 0049 7804-910 924

The Art of Living Indian Centers

VYAKTI VIKAS KENDRA, INDIA

List of Apex Bodies

VVKI - Andhra Pradesh Apex Body,
6-3-883/3, R.K. Plaza, Panjagutta,
Hyderabad - 500 002
Ph.: 040-23400782, 55218418
apapex@artoflivingindia.net
gsvprasad@hathway.com
All Districts of Andhra Pradesh

VVKI - Bihar Apex Body,
506-7, Sumati Place,
Boring Road Crossing, Opp.
Alankar Place, Patna-800001
Ph.: 0612-2520247, 2520232
biharapex@artoflivingindia.net
subhash_chandra@hotmail.com
All Districts of Bihar

VVKI - Chattisgarh -
Orissa Apex Body,
Probodha Apartments,
3rd Floor - E, Nageshwar Tangi,
Bhubhaneshwar - 751002
Ph.: 0671-2491819, 2491587,
2491816
choapex@artoflivingindia.net
All Districts of Chattisgarh and
Orissa

VVKI - Goa - Karnataka Apex
Body No. 19, 39th A Cross,
11th Main, IV T Block, Jayanagar,
Bangalore - 560 041
Ph.: 080-26645106, 080-26541424
gkapex@artoflivingindia.net,
vvkblr@vsnl.net
All Districts of Karnataka and the
State of Goa

VVKI - Gujarat Apex Body,
304, Silver Brooke Complex - A,
Opp. Doctor's House,
Near Parimal Crossing, Ellisbridge,
Ahmedabad - 380 006
Ph.: 079-6468395
gujarat@artoflivingindia.net
vvkgujarat@icenet.co.in
All Districts of Gujarat

VVKI - Jharkhand Apex Body,
402, Mangalam Apartments, 56,
Circular Road, Ranchi - 834 001
Ph: 0651-2562611,
Telefax : 0651-2260857, 2260557,
2260686
jharkhandapex@artoflivingindia.net
All Districts of Jharkhand

VVKI - Kerala Apex Body,
TC 6 / 1776 (2), "Schogini",
PTP - 292, Trivandrum - 695 038
Ph.: 0471-2360598
keralaapex@artoflivingindia.net
sree@schogini.com
All Districts of Kerala

VVKI - Madhya Pradesh Apex
Body, HIG 2/6, Gitanjali Complex
South T.T.Nagar, Bhopal
Ph.: 0755 - 2762784
Mobile: 9827264760 (Shrivastavaji)
mpapex@artoflivingindia.net
All districts of Madhya Pradesh

VVKI - Maharashtra Apex Body,
83, Nariman Bhavan, 8th Floor,
Mumbai - 400 021
Ph.: 022-22851118, 22851119
maharashtraapex@artoflivingindia.net
vvkimab@hathway.com
All Districts of Maharashtra

VVKI - North East Apex Body,
C/o Sri. Suresh Swami,
Gopal Restaurant Building,
Kamrup Chambers Road,
Fancy Bazaar, Guwahati - 781 001
Ph.: 0361-2606347 / 48 or
0361-2513675
neapex@artoflivingindia.net
Assam, Arunachal Pradesh,
Manipur, Meghalaya, Mizoram,
Nagaland, Tripura, Sikkim

VVKI - North India Apex Body,
C - 9, Green Park Extension,
New Delhi - 110 016
Ph.: 011-26562606, 011-26611301,
011-26611097
northapex@artoflivingindia.net
Punjab-Chandigarh, Delhi, Haryana,
Himachal Pradesh, Jammu &
Kashmir, Uttaranchal, Uttar
Pradesh

VVKI - Rajasthan Apex Body, B-11,
Mukharji Colony, Shastri Nagar,
Jaipur - 302 016
Ph.: 0141-201795, 094140-74380
(Sri. Gautam Mukherjee)
rajapex@artoflivingindia.net
All Districts of Rajasthan

VVKI - Tamil Nadu Apex Body, C/o
Atma Gnana Nilayam, #33,
Kalakshetra Road, Thiruvanmiyur,
Chennai - 600 041
Ph.: 044-24913702,
0431-3107398 (Sri. Kittu Rao)
tnapex@artoflivingindia.net
All Districts of Tamil Nadu

VVKI - West Bengal Apex Body,
No. 60, Mahanirban Road,
Kolkata - 700 029
Ph.: 033-24634676
wbapex@artoflivingindia.net
All Districts of West Bengal